Mindful Anger

Mindful Anger

A PATHWAY TO
EMOTIONAL FREEDOM

Andrea Brandt

with Brookes Nohlgren

W. W. NORTON & COMPANY

NEW YORK • LONDON

Copyright © 2014 by Andrea Brandt

For information about permission to reproduce selections
from this book, write to Permissions,
W. W. Norton & Company, Inc., 500 Fifth Avenue, New York, NY 10110

For information about special discounts for bulk purchases, please contact
W. W. Norton Special Sales at specialsales@wwnorton.com or 800-233-4830

Manufacturing by Quad Graphics Fairfield
Production manager: Leeann Graham

Library of Congress Cataloging-in-Publication Data

Brandt, Andrea.
Mindful anger : a pathway to emotional
freedom / Andrea Brandt. — First edition.
pages cm
Includes bibliographical references and index.
ISBN 978-0-393-70894-3 (hardcover)
1. Anger. 2. Meditation—Therapeutic aspects.
3. Mindfulness-based cognitive therapy. I. Title.
BF575.A5B73 2014
152.4'7—dc23
2013045077

ISBN: 978-0-393-70894-3

W. W. Norton & Company, Inc.
500 Fifth Avenue, New York, N.Y. 10110
www.wwnorton.com

W. W. Norton & Company Ltd.
Castle House, 75/76 Wells Street, London W1T 3QT

1 2 3 4 5 6 7 8 9 0

To JP, for your propensity to "make things better." It finally worked on this project! I love you.

Contents

Acknowledgments

First and foremost, I want to thank all of the people who have attended my anger workshops over the years. I have been inspired and educated by your courage and strength, and I am truly grateful to have been a part of your transformation.

And deep gratitude to my Wednesday night group and to all of my clients—I feel privileged to know you, to learn from you, and to be part of your journeys.

I am truly indebted to the many thinkers and experts in the field of anger who have influenced and informed my knowledge and expertise on this subject. I am particularly grateful to Pat Ogden at the Sensorimotor Psychotherapy Institute for her work with the body. You have allowed me to understand anger as a more healthy, productive, everyday emotion that doesn't have to be so scary or threatening.

I thank Brookes Nohlgren, a cherished writing partner on this project. I'm grateful for your ability to sift through loads of information and years of manuscripts to reveal my message and voice.

Also, I thank Kristin Vogelsong, one of the first people to have read the early drafts of this book and who very early on gave me insightful feedback and support.

Friends' and colleagues' unbelievable patience, insights, and loving support over the years helped me complete this book. You deserve my sincere gratitude and thanks for helping me through.

And I thank Fay Hove—level-headed, supportive, meticulous with great notes, and a loyal friend.

Introduction

When I was growing up, both of my parents repressed their anger. As a result, they were like two simmering volcanoes ready to blow at any moment. The explosion never came. Instead, I was treated with the kind of pervasive abuse that is harder to see than hitting or slapping but just as devastating. It was simply part of the fabric of the family environment.

My parents' marriage was deeply troubled, and my father was unfaithful. Threatened with losing him, my mother turned all her energy into keeping her only child close. Her anger came out in threats, tension, and complaints: "After all I've done for you, you treat me like this" was a particularly popular theme song. When her tongue was loosened by a few social drinks, my mother would criticize me for having close relationships with my grandmother or aunt—any connection that might challenge my ties to her. On the other hand, she was often too tired from work to give me the affection and fun experiences I so needed.

My anger mounted with each year, but, not surprisingly, my parents discouraged me from expressing and releasing it. I found ways to get back, nevertheless. For example, at 26, I briefly married a man I didn't love, mostly for the thrill of seeing my parents stage an elaborate and very costly wedding. They paid, but so did I. When I married Buzz, I was cut off from my feelings, living in my head—mostly intellectualizing my experiences. In the second year, Buzz decided to go into therapy, and soon, his psychologist suggested that I come in for my own sessions. I agreed to go, and it wasn't long before my then-husband and I were also in group therapy together.

One day in group, a man made a remark that triggered the repressed anger and frustration that I had been holding inside for so long. I don't even remember what he said to me, but I'll never forget my reaction. Suddenly I stood up, started screaming, and began swinging my purse around in the air. Seated on a couch across the room, Buzz was looking at me as if he wondered what kind of woman he had married—or whether his serene wife had somehow been replaced by this raging out-of-control twin.

I had become the erupting volcano. I totally lost control. I was so upset that I started for the door to leave the room, but the therapist insisted I stay. I did, only to break down in sobs. For four days afterward, I cried in the shower each morning. Not long after, Buzz and I divorced.

During this early experience with my anger, I didn't understand the best way to constructively express and release these feelings. Yet a lot of pent-up anger was released. As if struck by a lightning bolt, I was startled by the power of this event. I felt lighter, freer. I began to sense that there was value for me, and for others, in tapping into anger. As time went on, exploring my anger helped me to form healthy relationships, to engage people in a more genuine way, and to understand that I had value beyond work. In my family, achievement had been the only goal. I came to see that a lot more elements contributed to becoming a happy and well-rounded person. Anger, it turned out, wasn't a bad thing. Instead, it was the key to emotional freedom.

For me, the engine of this transformation was mindfulness, a thoughtful and intense focus on the present moment in which we allow sensations and feelings to reveal themselves without judgment. By quieting our mind, we can focus on the present and explore what our body, mind, and emotions are trying to tell us. This heightened state of awareness has long been practiced in many of the world's spiritual circles, and it is now being integrated into approaches to psychotherapy and taught as a practical life skill. Mindfulness is the number one tool required for breaking our negative anger habits and resolving the issues that cause anger in the first place. This opens the door to a richer appreciation of the cornucopia of emotions that can make life the rewarding experience it was meant to be, rather than a repressive monologue in which we often seem to be at war with the world.

LOOKING AT ANGER

My transformative experience provides examples of two expressions of anger. The shrieking, purse-swinging banshee who disrupted the therapy session may look more like anger, but the quiet, detached woman who walked in the door was equally angry and just as troubled. When anger comes out as rage, it is overtly destructive to the person's relationships and success in life. When anger is suppressed, it turns up as passive-aggressive and other self-defeating behaviors, habits, addictions, and even illness.

There are many ways we can respond to the feeling of anger. Most of them don't do us any good. Anger that is unleashed and out of control comes with a high price tag—both for ourselves and those we interact with—with consequences ranging from mild to severe. At its worst, we see the deadly results on the TV news each day—the violence of domestic abuse, terrorism, and school shootings. We watch as celebrities' rants and abusive tirades are caught on video and audio recordings, only to be replayed over and over again, threatening to damage or destroy their careers. Though most of us, thankfully, will never be touched by this height of violence, we all have within us the mechanism that makes this and other types of violence possible. Anger may come to us during a current experience or when thinking about the past. Often we get angry when things don't go our way or when we feel threatened.

We've all suffered the repercussions of acting out anger. When our behavior is angry, we damage that which is most valuable to us. We create distance in our relationships, crush our children's self-esteem, drive away business deals, erode our health, and undermine our own peace and well-being. None of us have gotten this far in life without giving or receiving some of these scars.

Perhaps this doesn't sound much like you. You really don't experience a lot of anger, and you never lash out. Maybe instead of expressing your anger outwardly, you stuff it all inside, where it feels safer and more manageable. Maybe you can't recall ever feeling anger at all. Is it possible that you've been spared this burden? No, not if you're human.

We all have anger. It's one of the most common of human emotions, so, if you're not feeling it, then you're probably unconsciously burying it instead. But anger that is buried isn't actually gone. Out of sight is rarely out of mind, and it certainly doesn't mean it no longer exists. In fact, hidden or covert anger may be just as damaging as the overt, outwardly destructive kind—only it wreaks havoc from the inside out. All sorts of physical and emotional problems can stem from suppressed anger: headaches, digestive problems, and insomnia, just to name a few. Cancer and heart disease, the leading causes of death in the United States, both have been linked to unresolved anger.[1]

Buried anger is lying in wait and will, when it can, resur-

---

1   Ed Susman, "Anger Drives Heart Attacks but Laughter May Be Antidote," Everyday Health, August 28, 2011, http://www.everydayhealth.com/heart-health/0829/anger-drives-heart-attacks-but-laughter-may-be-antidote.aspx; and Kristen Fischer, "Ticked Off? Your Serotonin Could Be Low," She Knows, November 3, 2011, http://www.sheknows.com/health-and-wellness/articles/845939/ticked-off-your-serotonin-could-be-low.

face. That's because anger is an emotion—a form of energy in motion, if you will. It is expressed in a continuum, with rage and aggression at the top, and frustration, annoyance, and irritation at the bottom, and everything else in between. If we view anger as an unacceptable emotion, we may decide that frustration, disappointment, and irritability, although not pleasant, are easier for ourselves and others to accept. Yet these more subtle forms of anger still prevent us from having fulfillment or joy in life. Although we're not openly expressing anger, it is leaking out all the time.

How do you know if you suffer from hidden anger? The best indicator may be what is not being seen. If you don't feel or experience anger somewhat regularly, you should consider the possibility that you fall into this group. To find out whether you do, in fact, have an anger problem, overt or covert, take a moment to answer a few key questions:

EXERCISE: GOT ANGER?

☐ 1. Are you angry much of the time? Are you abusive to others—verbally, emotionally, or physically—in your personal and business relationships?

☐ 2. Are you sarcastic or cynical about life, yourself, or others? Do your jokes demean others, mocking them and cutting them down?

☐ 3. Do you bully others to make yourself feel okay?

☐ 4. Once you've become angry, do you have trouble letting that anger go? Do you harbor resentments or hold a grudge?

☐ 5. Are you frustrated, disappointed, or irritable a lot, but without ever reaching the point of being angry?

☐ 6. Do you think that you're never angry? Are there times when you know a situation warrants being angry, but the emotion just doesn't come?

☐ 7. Do you feel powerless at times—hopeless in the face of even the smallest adversity and unable to take action for positive change? Do you feel like a victim of your circumstances much of the time?

☐ 8. Are you depressed frequently or for long periods of time?

☐ 9. Have you put important areas of your life on hold, thinking that you'll get to them someday and not consciously recognizing that you're not going to live forever?

If you answered yes to any of these questions, you have issues with anger, and you're dealing with it in a way that—at best—is limiting your emotional freedom and your enjoyment of life and—at worst—is damaging to yourself and others. Don't worry. You're not alone. Most of us have an unhealthy relationship to anger. We simply don't know what to do with this incredibly powerful emotion. That's why I've written this book—to help you understand your anger issues and learn how to deal with them effectively.

THE EMOTIONAL TOLL

The truth is that the way we deal with our anger has a powerful impact on how we experience all of our feelings, including love. If you're prone to acting out your anger, you probably recognize how that tends to push people away and create walls between you and the significant others in your life. If you're suppressing anger, the outcome is more subtle but no less real. By suppressing anger, we are covering our true feelings and our true self in layers of behavior that we think will keep the peace and avoid confrontation. Problem is, we're not letting others see the real self that deserves to be loved; intimacy is impossible without honesty and vulnerability.

Hidden anger can result in emotional and mental devasta-

tion. To avoid dealing with our feelings, we try to numb them—
with drugs and alcohol, overwork, or sexual promiscuity. We
will do just about anything and everything to keep ourselves
from feeling. Buried anger may also be the cause of other
seemingly unrelated problems, such as depression, apathy, laziness, insecurity, shyness, and passivity, which clearly rob us of
our zest for life.

You may be surprised to learn that depression can indicate
an anger problem that occurs when, instead of openly expressing anger, we turn that anger on ourselves. Sometimes, too,
depression results from "depressing," or pushing down, other
feelings including anger. Depression has other causes as well,
but if anger is at the root of it, then dealing with your anger will
alleviate the depression.

When we don't allow ourselves to feel our anger, we lose our
sense of self-esteem and self-respect. Many times, we just let
people walk all over us rather than tell them what we're feeling. We don't warn people when they've crossed the line and
stepped on our emotional toes. We don't let them know what
we need out of the relationship. We have trouble making decisions, and our personal connections lack intimacy. Let's face it,
part of intimacy is being honest, and we are not being honest if
we are not expressing what we truly feel.

A lot of what precedes anger is the inability to be honest. Few
people have grown up in an emotionally safe environment, a
place where they could be truthful about their feelings. Most
have gotten the message from their family that emotions, and
especially anger, are self-indulgent or embarrassing and best
kept to themselves.

The notion that many husbands can't deal with their wives'
emotionality is a cliché because it is so often true. I once coun-
seled a couple who could not bring themselves to talk about
anything upsetting. They spoke about work, household practi-
calities, and so on. The husband had no tools for speaking hon-

estly with his wife about her traits that upset him, so he would reveal his feelings to strangers: bartenders, online friends, and other strangers. This lack of honest communication is a recipe for disaster, creating an environment for emotional and even physical infidelity. It stands in the way of loving relationships.

When we get into the habit of disowning aspects of ourselves that we don't like, we limit and shortchange ourselves. If, for example, we don't want to be like our mother or father in some respect, we might disown a part of ourselves that resembles that parent. In doing so, we cut off our options, our energy, and our ability to honor some of the things about our parents that were good.

Michelle

One of my patients was very uncomfortable with her mother's behavior. In all of the mother's relationships with friends and family, she would behave in a consistently needy way. Watching this play out over the years, Michelle became convinced that any neediness was incredibly unappealing. She thought, "I never want to be needy and look like that. I'd rather shoot myself!"

Michelle made every effort as an adult to avoid any whisper of neediness. She started and owned a business, which she operated on her own. She had a daughter whom she raised by herself. There was no way that this woman was going to need help from anyone else—and no way she would take it.

Unfortunately, this conviction became an emotional deficit. Because she refused to open herself up to others, to be vulnerable, no one would open themselves up to her. One of the reasons her marriage ended was that whenever her husband offered help of any kind, she would say, "No, I'm fine." He began to feel that his presence wasn't significant in his wife's life, that she didn't actually care for him all that much.

Eventually, through therapy that used mindfulness as a primary tool, Michelle began to understand her pattern of neediness and not view it as a flaw. Asking for help honors the person you're asking and enables him or her to ask for help right back. When this woman started to allow a give-and-take in her relationship, she was able to heal the damage done during those closed-off years.

When we deny and run from our feelings, none of our nagging issues ever get resolved. Emotions don't just go away because we want them to. They reside in our psyche and have a life cycle of their own. When we have a physical wound, our bodies go through a series of healing steps. Blood vessels tighten to reduce blood flow, then platelets and clotting proteins rush in to seal the injury. White blood cells race to the scene to destroy any germs or toxins. Our bodies know exactly what to do to solve the problem.

Like the body, the psyche is innately programmed to heal. If emotions are not properly processed out, however, they become toxic and cause us serious harm. Therefore, they will keep showing up in our lives until we resolve them. They want to be healed. If we simply discharge or suppress the sensations and feelings related to emotions, nothing is resolved. By not addressing what we're actually angry about, the anger continues. The real issues don't get addressed. Progress is never made. We find ourselves running on a perpetual treadmill of emotions.

MINDFULNESS: ANGER IN, ANGER OUT

Practicing mindfulness means deliberately allowing your physical sensations and emotions to surface so that you can examine and release them. When I ask people to sit with their emotions—and that's just what I'll be asking you in the chapters to come—I know I am asking them to do something counterintuitive. But I also know that if you don't sit with it, the anger that may have formed in your childhood toward your parents is going to be transferred to your next relationship and then the next one, and so on. Unless you sit with your emotions, feel them through, and release them, they will cling to you and keep re-creating a scenario like the one where the feelings were originally generated. We have the choice of letting this angry energy move us into making choices that are good for us or just having it lead us back to destructive habits.

Anger that is not processed—not felt fully in the body as it happens, moved out through appropriate expression, and released—becomes stagnant in our emotional and physical systems and becomes toxic, causing us harm in every area of life. Energy, including the energy of emotions, has to go somewhere. If it is not processed and released, it will remain in our being, draining our life force and making it impossible for us to be fully present. It might seem surprising that holding on to certain kinds of energy can actually make you weak, but it's a common outcome.

We need to release the physical feelings associated with anger in order to let this emotion go. Remember, releasing anger does not mean venting or dumping, which can actually be a loss of control that comes from a lifetime of unprocessed anger. Nor is a release of anger a tamping down of emotions in an effort to get rid of them. "Anger in, anger out" expresses the full spectrum of healing because it is complete acceptance of this emotion. "Anger in" relates to recognizing the arrival of anger: becoming aware of it at the onset. This kind of awareness and recognition is accomplished through mindfulness. "Anger out" encompasses both the steps of expressing anger verbally in a constructive way and letting it soften and move the energy through our bodies.

Through mindfulness, you will learn to harness the physical impulse that seeks to short-circuit the emotional feeling of anger and prevent it from forming. This physical sensation, the body's fight-or-flight response, warns of a perceived danger and sets off a habituated reaction, which discharges or buries the anger immediately. Our job is to get curious enough about the origin of our anger so that we pay attention and make a different choice the moment we experience our body's instinctual reaction.

You might experience sadness or other surprising emotions, but you will also begin to see what you are truly angry about and whether the anger is covering up other emotions. By feeling those emotions—experiencing them and not burying them or trying to expel them—you will be able to let them go. An important by-product of letting feelings move through you is that you clear out your internal filter so you have room for new feelings. And that even goes for good feelings that you need to let go of. For example, how can you make room for a wonderful new love in your life if you are still holding on to an old love? Once you process a feeling, you can let it go, making room for new experiences. Mindfulness is the strategy for reaching this goal.

USING MINDFUL ANGER
TO ACHIEVE EMOTIONAL FREEDOM

The goal of this book is to get you back to being your true self—whole and complete, authentic and capable of experiencing all of your feelings, of fully giving and receiving love. With the simple tools of mindfulness, you can strengthen your connection with your inner world and learn to explore your anger, paying heed to the important messages it is sending. This will help you get your needs met in a much more harmonious and productive way. You can stop spending all of your time and life energy fearing or avoiding how you feel. You can become available not only to yourself, but also to those you love, truly giving them the emotional support they need to get through life's challenging moments. You can help others to accept their humanness and be free from the restriction of always having to please everyone else.

In order to stop—and reverse—the damage that anger can do to your relationships and to your life, it helps to understand your anger and the choices you have for dealing with it. The key to changing this pattern, to getting the upper hand on our emotional lives, is first becoming conscious of how anger works—gaining an awareness of what's happening, the part we play in it, and what other choices we might have to do something different. If everyone had this kind of awareness, plus the commitment to choosing other strategies to help them get what it is that they really want, we'd see a very different world on the nightly news.

We begin with the assessment. How does anger express itself in your life? Chapter 1 helps you answer that question. In Chapter 2, you will learn how anger can wrap your emotional life in chains, set the lock, and throw away the key. You'll see how much richer your life can be once you break those chains. Of course, you need the right tool. Chapter 3 provides some basic descriptions of mindfulness and some exercises that will allow you to put it to work for you.

In Chapter 4, you'll try out the mindfulness tools that will allow you to sit with the sensations and emotions that are triggered by your anger. Then, in Chapter 5, you'll see how to step in, assess what's happening, and release your anger in productive ways. Mindfulness also allows us to suspend our response until we've assessed the cause of our anger. As we see in Chapter 6, sometimes our anger is triggered by assumptions or ideas rooted in past experience. Approaching our anger mindfully can reveal those underlying thoughts and beliefs and put them to the test.

Like so many things, anger is learned at home. Chapter 7 takes us back to our childhood, where experiences in the family may have inflicted deep emotional wounds. Chapter 8 provides a five-step program to identify those wounds and unresolved anger so that we can learn and grow from our experiences. Having moved the anger out, we now have room for forgiveness and gratitude, described in Chapter 9, leading us toward a new life of emotional freedom and connection with others in Chapters 10 and 11.

This book is all about slowing down and exploring your anger when it is triggered instead of reacting to it out of habit. It's about honoring your anger as a beneficial emotion and learning what it has to teach you. It's about reintegrating the anger you cut off in childhood because it was unacceptable to feel back then. Reclaiming the cutoff parts of ourselves is beneficial and powerful, allowing us to live and love more fully. If we are disconnected from any part of our real experience, we can't fully take care of our own needs or be present to meet the needs of others.

The tools in this book will help you make changes that will improve every area of your life. Once you have learned to have a healthier response to your anger, not only will you become a more loving partner and parent, but your home will be happier, and the stage will be set for everyone to have a fuller and more rewarding life.

I also want to point out that it's important to have compassion for yourself as you work through your issues. Realize that you've done the best you could with the skills you had. It's not your fault if your childhood wasn't happy or if your family didn't provide what you needed. I repeat: It's not your fault if your childhood wasn't happy or if your family didn't provide what you needed. Don't beat yourself up because there are ways you need to change. Instead, pat yourself on the back for working on this now. Let's get started.

Mindful Anger

CHAPTER 1

The Anatomy of Anger

If you were asked to describe anger, you would probably talk about someone—adult or child—throwing a tantrum, with voice raised, arms waving, and face turning red. You might have someone in mind—a relative or friend or acquaintance who is always flying off the handle, even at a slight remark or action that annoys him. That is certainly an accurate picture of anger, but it is only one in a deck full of images that might represent anger.

Anger is still anger even when it simmers instead of boiling over. Another picture of anger might be someone who is critical and negative, someone who has a cynical response for everything you say; someone who always seems depressed and irritable. And if the anger is simmering low enough, the angry person might merely seem withdrawn from everyone, totally absorbed in television or computer games—or with emotions deadened by alcohol and drugs.

In this chapter, I give both styles of anger a close examination. Then, you'll have a chance to see where your behavior patterns fit.

ANGER STYLE 1: THE DUMPER/VENTER

Judy stopped her white Accord at the parking structure exit, looked out toward the street, and sighed. Before her was a steady stream of heavy traffic. "If I wait for a long break, I'll be here forever," she thought. Seeing a small opening in the flow, Judy stepped on the gas.

She had barely made the turn when persistent honking erupted from a black truck that had rushed up behind her on the boulevard. As the two vehicles moved along, the driver positioned his massive pickup uncomfortably close to Judy's Honda. He swerved his truck from side to side in their lane and flashed the truck's lights—as though he might run over her if she didn't get out of the way. When Judy turned right at the next stoplight, the truck rounded the bend, too, and soon, it was again just inches from the Accord's back bumper. Finally, Judy pulled to the side of the road and stopped, hoping that if she got out of his way, he would move on. Instead, he pulled to the curb at an angle, blocking her exit.

Watching to see if he would get out of the truck, she fumbled in her pocketbook for a cell phone. He rolled down the passenger window and shouted at her. "Dumb bitch!" the man growled, flashing her the finger. "Stay off the road!" Then, at last, he pulled away, and Judy breathed a sigh of relief. She felt sure the man had overreacted and behaved badly only to frighten her. He had succeeded.

Every day, people have upsetting road rage experiences with strangers, or they themselves fall prey to anger that explodes in this way. It's bad enough when this happens on the freeway, but an equivalent scene played out in your own living room with a family member is far more disturbing. If incidents in your home are looking more and more like episodes of the *Maury* or *Steve Wilkos* shows, you've obviously got some anger dumpers in your household. Could the anger dumper be you?

Anger dumpers will do anything but put a lid on it. Usually, everyone knows when dumpers are pissed off because they emphatically express it—dumpers scream, pace, and bristle—they may even shove, punch, pinch, bite, or kick others. Some dumpers will blast the nearest person with intense verbal abuse, delivered with animation at a high volume. Other dumpers will talk at a normal level, but their fury kills with criticism, shaming blame, and other stinging remarks.

Various therapists have referred to dumpers as "reactaholics" because these displays of anger can be retaliatory in intent. Triggered by frustration or a felt injustice, dumpers will react by propelling their anger at a target—at times, the person who was the source of their rage or, in other cases, just a convenient bystander. In some cases, a dumper's anger expresses a desire to gain power or dominance. They hurl their anger at others to achieve a goal or move an agenda forward.

If you could talk to dumpers about what's happening, they might tell you they become overwhelmed by uncomfortable feelings and are compelled to vent their anger. They might experience the anger as an energy that they just have to get out of their bodies. Most do not know how to stay with and tolerate angry feelings long enough to gain emotional clarity about what is making them angry or rationally choose the best actions to take in response. Their anger may be spewed endlessly as they talk on and on about the situation that triggered their feelings. To the recipient, the discharge of feelings can feel like a painful lecture.

Dumpers often make the mistake of thinking that when they dump angry feelings, they are dealing with issues or taking effective action. While anger can certainly serve as a prod to action, a dumper's expression of anger is often no more than an exercise in unloading feelings of fury on others. The real issues, particularly deeper or more subtle ones, can be missed entirely. Also, over time, people within the dumpers' firing range may figure out how to get around them or avoid them completely. Additional consequences for dumpers are lost relationships, loneliness, and a lack of emotional support.

Do You Dump Your Anger?

Are you unclear about whether you fit into the anger dumper profile? The questions below will help you get a better take on it.

- Are you easily angered?
- Are you frequently drawn into situations that escalate into anger?
- Do you express your anger before thinking it through?
- Do you become furious when you're interrupted or blocked from a goal?
- Do you go over an issue, or triggering event, again and again in your mind, almost to the exclusion of thinking of anything else?
- Do you get angrier the longer you ponder a provoking situation?
- Do you have difficulty letting go of a dispute?
- Do you respond with anger when criticized?
- Do you sometimes just act angry in order to get your way?
- Do you enjoy the intense feelings of anger?
- Are you angry much of the time?
- Do you explode with anger, and then later ask yourself, "What just happened?"
- Are your episodes of anger related to strongly held beliefs about what others should do?
- Do you lose control when you're angry—raising your voice, slamming your hand against the table, throwing whatever is handy?
- Have you harmed or lost valued relationships because of your anger?
- Do you use your anger to silence and control others?

- Do you identify being angry as just a part of the way you are?
- Does your anger bring on physical symptoms such as a tightness and throbbing in your chest, headaches, or indigestion?

The general anger dumper category includes five substyles with interesting variations. Let's take a look at these anger patterns now. As you read about the five dumper substyles, note that there's usually one pattern an anger dumper will identify with most. However, you may see aspects of another substyle in his or her anger behavior as well.

1. Anger as a Defense Against Shameful Feelings

These anger dumpers have a lingering feeling of being not good enough. Their belief is that they're flawed human beings. Most grew up in families that didn't make them feel special or important. Now they use anger to keep others at a distance. These dumpers don't want anyone to notice all the stuff that's making them feel ashamed. Deeply sensitive to criticism, they'll become pissed off over innocent remarks or mere suggestions for improvement. Although the dumpers push family, friends, and coworkers away with their anger, they may not realize how far people are willing to go to avoid them. Sadly, they can become isolated. Because their parents' attention was lacking or inconsistent, these individuals fear abandonment. At the slightest sign of a snub, they'll reject someone before that person has a chance to reject them—increasing the feelings of isolation.

Charlie

Charlie's father always went overboard in dishing out physical discipline. His punishments far exceeded the mistakes Charlie and his brother made. These experiences left Charlie with deep feelings of shame and low self-worth that remained with him into marriage and fatherhood.

One night after their children were in bed, Charlie's wife, Darla, suggested that she and her husband play a new board game she'd picked up while shopping for their son's birthday present. When Charlie lost the first round, he angrily pushed the board and game pieces to the floor. Growling that it was a stupid game, he rushed out the door to go drinking at a local bar. When Charlie got back in the wee hours of the morning, Darla pretended to be asleep. The next night, Charlie told her that he had thrown the board game away.

2. Anger Used Repeatedly to Manipulate Others

Bullies use intentional anger relentlessly to harass others. In the past, these anger dumpers learned that anger was a great way to make people do what they wanted. This may have started in childhood, if Mom always gave in when the bully threw a tantrum. At times, these bullies will decide on impulse to pretend to be angrier than they really are. In other instances, they actually plan their anger strategically in advance to manipulate someone through guilt, especially a child. Suppose Dad knows that little Bobby is going to want him to play ball in the backyard after work, when all he wants to do is pop open a beer and watch sports on TV. He may walk in the door and explode about the bike Bobby left in the driveway. That way, Bobby runs off, and Dad gets to keep his preferred agenda. Before an anger attack, you may hear this type of dumper say something like, "I guess I just have to put a little pressure on 'em."

These dumpers are into power, control, and dominance. They like to be feared. Scaring people by acting furious can even seem funny to them. "You should have seen the look on his face when I raised my hand," they'll tell friends. All the while, they are aware of what they're doing. Their anger is purposeful—to achieve certain ends—and it may include physical violence as a manipulative tool.

3. Being Angry as a Bad Habit

For these dumpers, anger is a way of life. They're angry every day of the week—and they often don't know why. Usually, there's a deep unresolved issue in their personal history, and the animosity is a sign that they're still hurting. Their anger serves as a shield that covers up the pain. These individuals start the day in a foul mood that doesn't lift as the hours pass. Being negative and angry feels normal to them. Their pessimism runs deep, and they will expect things to go wrong. Over time, you'll see them throw a lot of tantrums.

4. Anger Based on Judgments and Moral Superiority

In these cases, dumpers feel entitled to their anger. They're self-righteous and believe that the actions of others are morally wrong. When other people's behavior disappoints them, they feel superior. Their goal is to get other people to do things the right way. They're almost always ready for a fight. These individuals tend to alienate others with all their judgments. But there's no guilt because, in their way of thinking, it's all for a good cause. These dumpers may base their judgments on grounds that are religious, political, or familial—any area in which they're sure they know best.

5. The Dumper Who Seeks an Adrenaline Boost or Rush of Anger

Some anger dumpers have a limited emotional range, and anger is one of their few notes. They get a high from the physical sensations that come with being furious—including the quicker heartbeat, more rapid breathing, and increased alertness. Over time, their tolerance for anger increases, and they need even more vigorous interactions with others in order to feel excitement about being alive, just like the alcoholic needs more and more alcohol to get a buzz on or to repress feeling.

Like other addictive elements, anger can eventually take over and gain control of a dumper. If this occurs, it may lead to very dangerous territory as the dumper loses control over when the anger erupts and in what form. Screaming encounters can turn into physical clashes with fists flying, or worse.

ANGER STYLE 2: THE WITHHOLDER/SUPPRESSOR

Keith and Stacey

Keith eased his BMW into the garage, arriving back home after running Saturday morning errands. On the passenger seat, a pile of movies on DVD waited for him. All Keith wanted to do was unwind at the townhouse that weekend, and he was enjoying the thought of a few hours alone with his wife, Stacey, while their two young sons were attending a schoolmate's birthday party.

Stacey, however, had other plans. "Keith, the home association mixer starts in half an hour," she announced as he trudged into the kitchen. "You have just enough time to take a shower and change."

"Oh, I forgot," Keith said, owning up to it. "Listen, I'm really beat. You know how hard I've been working. Let's skip it and hang out at home this afternoon, okay?"

Stacey stared at her husband for a long moment. "No

way," she finally responded. "If you're not going, you're staying here alone. Got it?"

Without a word, Keith left her and bolted into the living room with the DVDs. "Why are these people more important than me?" he wondered to himself. "Doesn't she understand that I want time with her, and that I'm too exhausted to go out again?" But instead of sharing his feelings with Stacey, Keith kept his thoughts to himself. He went to the mixer, but his thoughts were on his growing resentment. While others talked around him, he reviewed a catalog of instances when he had given up what he needed in order to keep the peace.

Keith is a classic anger withholder. Believing that anger is destructive and should be avoided, he is shunning a conflict of needs that is calling out to be addressed. Anger withholders choose not to express their anger directly, and there are subtle distinctions in how this occurs in different people. As with anger dumpers, there are some noticeable subpatterns.

1. Detachment From Anger

Some people are so cut off from their anger that they have no conscious awareness of it. They are likely to be highly skilled at deflecting the anger (and probably most of their emotions) on a very deep psychic level. Detached people don't realize when someone has hurt them or pissed them off. They walk through life numb, in a kind of trance. It's as if their intake channels have been muted so that they never hear the message to be angry.

2. Anger That Is Recognized but Not Directly Expressed

Other anger withholders are conscious of their anger and feel it building up inside. However, they choose to conceal it. When they find themselves feeling very angry, they "get out of Dodge," either mentally or physically—turning on the TV, going to the bathroom, even leaving the house to take a walk. They fear how the anger will express itself, worry about the consequences, or believe that expressing their anger is wrong. Some people in this category have a large investment in being nice and looking good. Since they're holding so much in, these withholders can be very rigid and feel stiff as a board when you hug them. All that repressed anger may ooze out in passive-aggressive types of behavior, as they act out their anger indirectly. The withholder might also fall into a "stuff and blow" pattern—eventually erupting and jumping from the anger withholder to the anger dumper category—what I call style 1.5 below.

Dolores and Fred

Dolores and Fred had been married for 10 years. When she lost her job after their marriage and decided to stay home, he was annoyed at her lack of contribution to the relationship, but he kept it to himself. Then she was diagnosed with breast cancer. He knew she was looking to him for support, but he was scared about the possibility of losing her, and he had never been comfortable around sick people. It seemed to him that she was getting more than her fair share of benefits from their marriage, but he kept that to himself. For her part, Dolores was hoping to have Fred by her side during the difficult times she was facing.

As part of her treatment, Dolores had to do four rounds of chemotherapy. Fred would take her to the hospital every Thursday. Instead of sitting with her—she had told him family could stay during the infusions—he would watch television in the waiting room. By Friday morning, she was usually feeling pretty sick, but Fred had to work, didn't he? Otherwise, who would pay for her treatments? Dolores understood, and she was able to manage on her own, but she hoped to have his company on weekends. Fred had always played golf with some friends on Saturday, however, and he saw no reason to break his routine. Sometimes he stayed out afterward and had dinner and drinks with some of his buddies. As he saw it, he was doing her a favor—cooking smells in the house would make her even sicker. From her point of view, she was being abandoned when she most needed help. Sunday, Fred stayed home, but even then, they didn't talk. Fred always found chores to do around the house or sports to watch on TV. He encouraged her to stay in bed and get some rest when what she really wanted was company. Fred never complained to Dolores or raised his voice; instead, he used passive-aggressive behavior to make her feel bad.

3. Substituting Anxiety for Anger

In our culture, it's much more acceptable to show anxiety than anger. So one of the things people do is let anxiety take the place of their angry feelings. The anxiety is actually a defense against owning up to their fury. For example, someone may be angry at a parent for abandonment or a partner for not meeting her needs, and she is afraid to express it for fear of threatening the relationship. As a result, rage may be transformed into anxiety—jumpiness, racing thoughts, constant motion, excessive worry. To find out if this third withholding pattern fits you, the next time you feel really anxious, check in with yourself and explore the nervous feelings. Breathe and let your feeling rise up and evolve. See if the nervousness leads to anger or maybe also to sadness.

4. Disowning Anger and Assigning It to Someone Else

Disowned anger is sometimes referred to as paranoid anger. These anger withholders don't recognize their own anger and instead feel that others are angry at them. They'll project their anger out and see it as coming toward themselves from other people. Often, these withholders unconsciously do something to provoke anger in the people they're dealing with. Then, feeling vulnerable to attack, they believe they need the power boost of their anger to protect themselves. People with paranoid anger frequently feel like victims in situations, not aware that they provoked the conflict. This general anger pattern is seen in people dealing with authority figures, such as children relating to parents or employees interacting with bosses.

5. Repeatedly Stuffing Anger in a Chronic Victim Pattern

To hold on to their relationships, chronic victims will accept anything from others. The thought of risking loss of a relationship by expressing anger is just too frightening. These anger withholders frequently turn their ire on themselves. They either take the blame for other people's behavior, figure that they don't deserve any better, or come up with excuses for their victimizers. In these ways, they give people permission to dump all over them. If only the chronic victims would allow themselves to explore and express their anger, they could learn how to stand up for their rights. These withholders can become passive-aggressive as well.

Beth

Beth was bending over backward in an attempt to understand her husband Norm's need to be there for his ex-wife, Karen, and the children from that earlier marriage. Karen had full-time custody of the two kids. Norm's efforts to help included several visits a week to Karen's home and numerous phone calls each day, supposedly for emergencies. Beth was sympathetic to Karen and all her responsibilities. However, the reality was that Norm's attention to the other household had begun to hurt his new marriage.

Norm was ignoring many of Beth's needs out of guilt over the divorce and leaving his children. Beth just put up with her husband's behavior, telling herself that things would improve with time. Meanwhile, Norm had no idea how hurt and angry Beth really felt; she wasn't even acknowledging it to herself, much less telling him about it. By chronically excusing and rationalizing Norm's behavior, Beth allowed these patterns to continue. She wasn't talking to Norm about finding a balance for where he was putting his energy.

As you can see, there are many ways that we might end up not claiming our anger. In fact, you may find that you slide into different methods of withholding at different times. Usually, however, as with the anger dumper style, there is one predominant pattern for a particular withholder.

Interestingly, one of my patients used to be so distanced from her anger that she called her agitated self an evil twin. I reminded the patient that this was not a separate person, but an actual part of her. This shows how much we fear and avoid our angry feelings and actions. It's amazing how far we'll go. At times, it seems that we'll do just about anything not to feel angry. Here are a few of the typical things that anger withholders do:

1. Become buried in work or projects.
2. Eat way too much.
3. Get absorbed in TV shows or movies.
4. Play on the computer.
5. Withdraw from others and sulk.

6. Escape into exercise.

7. Go on a shopping spree (when life gets tough, the tough go shopping).

8. Blast music.

9. Take on too much responsibility for other people's problems—it's a great way to make yourself feel burdened, when the others never asked for your help in the first place.

10. Criticize yourself or feel guilty instead of experiencing your anger.

11. Become passive about pursuing goals or making other life improvements.

12. Drinking and substance abuse.

13. Smother feelings with depression.

All of these avoidance methods block the basic message that anger tries hard to deliver—that something is wrong and needs to be dealt with. Zoning out in these ways may seem easier in the short run than allowing our anger to surface. But as a habitual pattern, such a strategy can have a high price. If we try to avoid our feelings, we can develop other, quite serious problems—depression, anxiety, passivity, ill health, and many other limits on our joy and aliveness. The result can be just as devastating to our life and family as dumping our anger.

In order to get the important message that anger is trying to deliver, withholders need to steer clear of the typical avoidance habits and let this inner communication come through.

CAUGHT IN BETWEEN: STYLE 1.5

It's interesting to note that anger dumpers may once have been anger withholders. Certain people will hold their anger in for so long (possibly for years) that it eventually becomes too toxic for their bodies and suddenly explodes outward. These dumpers will overreact to minor things—perhaps all the time. Some people alternate between withholding and dumping.

This type of dumper may try to avoid or deny anger for a while, using any diversion to keep it at bay—for example, playing computer games excessively. Because of the effort of holding so much angry energy inside, they may seem cranky, irritable, or impatient. Sooner or later, however, they can't take it anymore, and the anger will pour out in a massive eruption— like Mount Vesuvius on that fatal day. During the episode, the dumper loses control and will ferociously shout and carry on. Victims are left to drown in all the toxic energy that was just spewed upon them.

Often, the dumper's reaction is way out of proportion to the triggering event. That's because he or she is not just reacting to the here and now but also to all the unaddressed events that have piled up. Later, the dumper may wonder what happened and feel guilty about the angry episode. Some people in this category dump their anger more frequently than others. While this pattern has withholding aspects, these individuals eventually dump their anger with gusto.

WHICH STYLE ARE YOU?

Now that we've covered the two primary anger styles, it's time for you to begin identifying where you see yourself within these broad patterns of reactions. The following exercises will progressively help you to become aware of your primary style for reacting to anger and to discover where you learned it and how it has been affecting your life. This type of awareness makes change possible. I urge you to create an anger journal for yourself, either buying a notebook or setting aside a place in your favorite digital device. Your anger journal will become a record of your work with this book, and it will be a history of your progress toward emotional freedom.

EXERCISE: WARMING UP:
JOURNALING FOR SELF-DISCOVERY

Gaining insight into our lives requires self-reflection. It is the foremost method for understanding ourselves and making lasting change. It's also not always easy at first, especially when what we'd like to examine about ourselves is fueled with an emotional charge. This book is full of concepts and exercises to prompt self-reflection—that's what mindfulness is all about. To ease you into this immensely beneficial practice so you can discover more about your anger, we're going to start out with a simple exercise that will allow you to take a step outside of yourself and gain the perspective of a more neutral observer. Then, once you have gained a little experience with exploring your anger, you will have a greater awareness with which to identify your anger style.

1. With your journal in hand, find a quiet place where you won't be disturbed, and seat yourself in a comfortable position. When you're ready to begin, take several slow, deep breaths.

2. Once you feel relaxed, allow your mind to wander to a time recently when you became angry or had a strong emotional reaction that you suspect might be related to anger.

3. As you recall the event, jot down in your journal a few lines describing it in as much detail as possible: What happened? Who was there? What did you and any others who were there do and say? How did the interaction end?

4. Now, setting your journal aside, close your eyes. Take a few more deep breaths and then review the event again, only this time visualize it on the screen of your mind. Picture yourself and any others who were present. Pay special attention to each individual's body language and notice how it reveals the person's state of mind. What does a person's words and actions reveal about their

emotions and thoughts? Just watch the scene neutrally as it unfolds, as if you were watching a movie. When the event is over, open your eyes.

5. Add to your journal anything new you noticed about your experience and participation in the event: your thoughts, feelings, words, and behaviors. Add anything else that reviewing the event now brings to mind.

6. When you're finished journaling about that scenario, allow your mind to move to another recent, emotionally provoking event. Repeat Steps 1–5 for it and as many other events as you like.

Once you have examined several instances of anger in your recent past, you will be ready to identify your anger style in the next exercise.

EXERCISE: YOUR STYLE— DUMPER OR WITHHOLDER?

This exercise details different ways of expressing anger. Characteristics of anger dumpers are listed with numbers. Qualities of anger withholders are listed with letters. As you read through the list, write down in your anger journal the number or letter of any characteristic that is part of your behavior; then add a few lines about how that behavior occurs in your life.

ANGER DUMPER

1. You're constantly angry. Your angry feelings show up in all areas of your life. That's just how it is for you.
2. You stay angry for long periods. It's difficult to let go of your anger.
3. "Cynical" is your middle name. You make a joke of everything, even if you hurt someone else's feelings.

4. You're angry and you feel it's justified. The most important thing is your latest cause or your judgment that others are not doing what they should be. You think less of those who don't seem to care as much.

5. You're a bully. Anger is how you get others to do what you want.

6. Your anger is just below the surface, unexpressed, but noticeable to others through a consistent energy emanating from you.

ANGER WITHHOLDER

A. You don't get angry. This is not an emotional experience that you can identify with. Still, you suspect you should.

B. You're aware of your anger but don't dare express it. Though you can feel your anger getting ignited, you find an indirect way to handle the issue. You believe that expressing your anger is wrong.

C. Feeling frustrated and irritable is the norm for you; however, your anger never seems to break through.

D. Life depresses you. The person you're most angry at is yourself.

E. You feel like you're always the victim—that others take you for granted or take advantage of your good nature. Still, anger feels like too much effort. What difference would it make?

F. You speak so softly that others have difficulty hearing you—you're using voice to control your feelings.

If you've written down mostly numbers, you are an anger dumper. If you've written down mostly letters, you are an anger withholder. Take a few minutes to reflect on what you've learned, and make some notes in your journal.

THE IMPACT OF YOUR ANGER
ON YOURSELF AND OTHERS

Many people who come to me for therapy and attend my anger workshops are not fully aware of the impact their unhealthy responses to anger are having across their lives. They are often in denial or at least minimize their anger style's effects. But this only keeps them stuck. Coming to terms with the reality of our choices can be an extremely powerful motivator that propels us toward positive change. Therefore, in the following exercise, I encourage you to use your anger journal to explore some of the most significant consequences your anger style has had on your life.

EXERCISE: WHAT IS THE COST OF ANGER?

1. To begin, think of the different areas where acting out your anger in your unique way has, or at least you suspect may have, had an impact. Write about the area in your journal, along with a few notes about what you do in that situation. Below are some general categories, but feel free to add your own or to make them more specific.
   - Relationships
   - Career
   - Health
   - Social life
   - Daily activities
   - Personal development
   - Peace of mind

   For example, on which relationships has your anger style had an impact? With your spouse or mate, kids, parents, coworkers, boss, friends, neighbors?

2. Next, evaluate and rate the severity of the impact of the angry venting or withholding on the areas you listed. Use the scale below to record a number for it in your journal. For example, your impatience and continual, low-level irritability causes

   1 = Minor or infrequent problems
   2 = Moderate or occasional problems
   3 = Severe or many problems

   Once you've assigned each a rating, add any other information that may bring you further insight into the situation.

3. Finally, to evaluate the consequences of your angry behavior accurately, you're going to need to be objective enough to see all of the results of your anger style. This means not only the costs but also the accomplishments or gifts. Did this particular pattern of addressing your anger help you to meet a need? For example, if an angry outburst stopped someone from upsetting you but also pushed that person away entirely, you can see that the method of handling the anger kept you safe but also kept you alone and unable to connect with someone else. As another example, did you manage to keep the peace by swallowing your anger, but as a result end up not getting your own needs met?

4. Make sure that in completing this exercise, you have written about at least three consequences, being sure to include for each (1) the area of life affected, (2) the cost, (3) the gift or accomplishment, if any, (4) the level of impact, and any other details.

At best, you have acted out anger in ways that have been limiting you; at worst, you have been harming your relationships and well-being. Either way, the most important thing to understand is that you are not a bad person. While it's okay to recognize your faults, you have to put aside your judgments and just keep your eye on the ball—toward finding and using the tools that will help you do something that you can feel proud of. In the next chapter, we will learn more about anger and the gifts (yes, you read that right) that it can bring to your life.

CHAPTER 2

The Key Role of Anger in Emotional Freedom

Anger is bad. That's one of the earliest lessons we learn from our caregivers and society, as they point to the loud, raging, sometimes violent explosions that are the main caricature of anger. Because anger is an uncomfortable energy in our bodies, we tend to think they must be right. The thing is, this is one case in which our parents and other teachers are totally wrong. You see, angry behavior is just the last episode in an often quick-moving series of events: the triggering action or gesture or word, the feeling we get in response to that trigger, and the way we choose to respond. Fearful of being overtly angry, most people respond by stuffing their anger inside, thinking that it can't do any harm there. Once again, they're wrong.

Anger is good. In fact, anger is an instrument of great benefit to your happiness rather than being its executioner. Most people are not aware of the critical difference between the emotion of anger—a physical experience in our bodies that is not destructive but actually gives us important information we need to make good decisions—and the destructive behavior that follows the emotion of anger. Emotions are reactions in the body that directly connect to our thoughts. They demonstrate the connection between the mind and the body. As an emotion, anger brings us important messages about our internal feelings and our external environment.

In this chapter, we're going to see how using our anger can

contribute to our emotional freedom and help us live with more joy and less guilt.

ANGER ISN'T A BAD THING— AND NEITHER ARE YOU

The first thing I'd like you to know is that behaving badly when you're angry doesn't mean that you are bad. Your response to anger doesn't define you as a person. This is true even if you are at the extreme end of the spectrum—verbally or physically abusive to others. But you're also not off the hook. Somewhere inside us, we all know right from wrong. We know that we don't have the right to act out our anger against others. We have a personal responsibility to learn to handle and communicate our anger in a safe and productive way.

When you separate yourself from your actions, you make a space for new and better choices. To start, it can be helpful to recognize where your anger patterns began. After all, you learned them somewhere—you weren't born with an unhealthy response to anger.

Most of us learned how to express our anger in our family of origin—both from watching the way our parents handled their anger and from the direct and implicit messages they gave us about how we should handle our own. In Chapter 1, you examined the way you deal with your anger. Now let's reflect on whether you witnessed these same patterns in the household where you grew up. Use your anger journal so that your findings become part of your journey toward emotional freedom.

EXERCISE: FINDING YOUR ANGER GENES

1. In your journal, find the pages where you listed the ways you express your anger. Now think about your parents and other significant people in your early life.

2. Place an M for Mother next to the numbers or letters that describe how your mother behaved when she was angry.

3. Place an F for Father next to the numbers or letters that describe how your father behaved when he was angry.

4. Place the initials of other important people in your life next to the numbers or letters that describe how they behaved when they were angry.

5. Take a look at what you've discovered. How many of your anger behaviors or habits also belonged to another person in your early life?

6. What did you learn from these others about how to express your own anger?

When you understand how you came to adopt certain behaviors, you begin to see that you have the choice, and the ability, to change them. You can learn something new that will be of much greater benefit to you. Once you realize that you aren't inherently bad, flawed, or screwed up in some way, you can begin to free yourself from the grip of your habits and start making new choices by your own design.

The second important thing to know is that anger isn't bad either. The distasteful and often destructive behaviors that we erroneously designate as anger are not anger at all, but our efforts to contain or avoid the sensations or emotions that we feel when our anger is triggered. The fuming, spewing, and suppressing we have come to think of as anger are actually our responses to anger. In between the emotion and the behavioral response, we can find a treasure trove of information about what's happening inside of us. Instead of ignoring our anger or letting it explode pointlessly, we'll learn to welcome anger and the messages it brings.

DON'T GET RID OF YOUR ANGER—USE IT

As a therapist, I'm not trying to help people get rid of their anger. On the contrary, I want them to use it for all it's worth. There isn't an area of our lives—relationships, careers, health, you name it—that wouldn't improve with proper handling of our anger. When people learn how to respond to their anger, they can reap the goodness it has to offer. This is so important that I can honestly say that I can't see people getting through life successfully without knowing how to use their anger constructively. Sadly, this is one lesson we rarely learn in childhood.

Anger serves us in several specific ways. Because the body often gives us signals when the mind is unaware of a problem, it is an important channel to listen to in order to understand our present state of being. By becoming aware of what our body is telling us through anger, we can more effectively understand ourselves and be much more proactive in taking care of ourselves. This, plus using the energy of anger as a power boost to operate more assertively in the world, can shift us out of a victim state and give us the initiative to create the life we want. Finally, since anger is a mechanism for knowing and communicating our truth, it becomes an important avenue for improving relationships, both with others and with ourselves. Intimacy requires safety, and safety is created when our needs are met and our boundaries are strong. The self-awareness that can be gained through the feeling and processing of anger provides a foundation for the honesty and trust that give us the safety we need to let our guards down and become vulnerable and open to intimate relationships.

Exploring our anger makes us look at our values, needs, boundaries, and belief systems and ask, "What's going on here? Is this working for me? Does something need to change to better align my actions to what I truly want? How can I arrange this better? What is in everyone's best interests?"

Anger has a wealth of information for us if we are committed to listening.

A SIGNAL THAT SOMETHING IS WRONG

Anger is an indicator that something is wrong, and its energy fuels us to action. The key, of course, is knowing enough about how anger works and then exploring it to find out what is wrong so you can figure out the best way to correct the problem. That's the task you will accept as you move forward in this book.

If you find yourself acting out—drinking too much, starting arguments, having an affair, or shaming someone else—or if you experience a physical response that indicates anger, such as clenching your jaw or fist, your smartest move is to pause and ask, "What's going on here? What is my jaw or fist trying to say?" There is tremendous benefit in anger if you can find out what it has to teach you about what isn't working in your life. We'll look at two similar situations with very different responses.

Suzanne and Kipper

Suzanne runs a freelance editing business out of her home. She's in the middle of a project when her 10-year-old son, Kipper, interrupts, asking about lunch. "Go make yourself a sandwich," Suzanne hollers. "You're big enough to take care of yourself now! I need some peace and quiet here, or there won't be any food for you to eat!"

Kipper withdraws, but Suzanne now finds herself so charged with anger that she can't get her mind back on the job. She closes her eyes, takes a couple of deep breaths, and realizes that she overreacted to Kipper's request.

Still, the anger is real. What could be wrong? Her anger could be telling her that she feels pressured by a deadline.

Then she hears her words to Kipper and realizes that she is afraid for her family's financial security, which is based on her job performance.

She finds Kipper in the kitchen making a sandwich, gives him a hug, and apologizes. They sit down for lunch together.

Feeling herself overwhelmed by anger, Suzanne takes a moment to evaluate the origin of her anger. She realizes that Kipper's interruption is not what she's really angry at. Suzanne sees herself as a self-confident, capable provider for her family. The demands of her current job are crossing the boundaries of that identity.

Now let's look at a similar scenario with a different outcome.

Wilma and Max

Wilma stretches out on the couch in the living room with a book. She's just gotten comfortable when 10-year-old Max, who was supposed to be next door playing with his friend, comes in and turns on the TV.

"Max!" she shouts. "Mommy is reading now. You're supposed to be outside playing. God knows, you need the fresh air and exercise. Now, get out of here and play." Max runs out of the room, leaving the TV on. Leaping off the couch, Wilma grabs the remote, turns the TV off, and throws the remote at the wall.

"Why can't he ever leave me alone?" she shouts. She never realized that being a mother would be so exhausting. Didn't she deserve some time to herself? After all, her mother was never available when she came home from school—always playing cards, or on the phone, or doing her nails, or just watching TV. Isn't that how things are supposed to be?

If Wilma took the time to think about her angry outburst, she might remember how lonely she was in those
hours between the end of school and the time her father
came home. As it happens, Max has quarreled with his
friend, and he needed to talk to somebody about it. The
little girl Wilma once was could identify with that feeling.
No matter what concerns she brought home from school,
her mother never wanted to chat with her. Sometimes, she
would talk to herself, just for the company.

Wilma's anger at her son is a reflection of her own relationship with her mother. Wilma had learned never to interrupt
her mother. Somehow, she also picked up the idea that everything is always supposed to go Mommy's way—an inaccurate
and otherwise limiting belief she has carried into her own adult
life. For someone with this belief, an interruption while she is
concentrating is a boundary breach.

In the first anecdote, Suzanne examines her anger and
decides that giving attention to her child when he needs it is
more important to her than her work deadline. If she explores
her anger further, she might consider whether she is putting
unreasonable demands on herself in terms of her work. Perhaps there are other ways to support her family without experiencing so much stress. Her anger can help her make positive
steps forward in her life.

In the second anecdote, Wilma allowed her anger to explode
without attending to its message. Having unconsciously adopted
the set of expectations she learned from her own mother, she
mindlessly behaves in the same way. If she connected with the
little girl who longed for connection with her mother, she
might understand what her son is feeling and begin to forge a
bond with him.

It's not just a question of how they handled their anger. Both
women started by venting their feelings. Then Suzanne looked

for the message and apologized to Kipper, reassuring him of her affection and the important role he plays in her life. By ignoring Max, Wilma increased her distance from her child and lost an opportunity to build closeness.

ANGER: DEFENDING YOUR BOUNDARIES

For both Suzanne and Wilma, anger rose when a personal boundary was being crossed. This is one of the consistent messages that anger will deliver: "Look out! You're being threatened." At the most basic level, this involves the safety of our body. All of us, however, also have a sense of self or ego identity, cobbled together from our family background, our experience in school, our geographical location, our likes and dislikes, our role in the family, and our role in life. To feel safe in the world means not having our physical and ego boundaries threatened.

Because healthy boundaries are so important to our well-being, any violations are disruptive to energy and balance. Anger is the red flag that warns us if there is a threat, so that we can either protect ourselves or repair the injury. The method of response and repair depends on the type of threat. Let's look at some examples.

Safeguarding the Body

I often ask my therapy patients to stand facing me in one spot in the room. Then I walk toward them and ask them to tell me when I have gotten too close and they start to feel uncomfortable. This helps them become aware of their physical boundaries. It also allows them to experiment with how much intimacy and closeness they can tolerate. Knowing ourselves better helps our relationships, and knowing ourselves includes knowing our boundaries: what we can tolerate and what does and doesn't feel good to us.

When we experience a physical threat, our body feels the fight-or-flight response. Developed way back in human evolution, this phenomenon helped humankind to become master of the food chain—and not someone else's meal. In brief, the fight-or-flight response ensures that all of the body's energy is diverted to survival. We can experience this reaction to psychological threats, too. Since, as a species, early humans survived better in groups, we had to cooperate with one another and thus developed certain rules for interacting. Behaving in a way that got us expelled from the tribe would put our lives at risk. This made us very sensitive to our interactions with others, and the slightest displeasure or affront by someone else could trigger our fight-or-flight response. Thus experiencing even a tiny psychological or physical threat—such as rudeness or a sudden loud noise—sets the body into action. And with continual stress, scientists have found, we experience ailments like high blood pressure, heart disease, substance abuse, ulcers, weight gain, cancer, and accelerated aging. Our most primary boundary is our physical self, which explains why experiencing any sexual or physical abuse can be so damaging psychologically.

Safeguarding the Ego

In addition to the physical body, we also have a more subtle aspect of self that is our ego or self-image. Our self-image includes how we see ourselves, what aspects of ourselves are most connected to our self-worth, and what we love about life. When the things we value in ourselves and in our world are threatened or treated with disrespect, an important boundary is breached. Something is wrong, and our body-mind responds— we get angry.

This response can also be traced back to evolutionary psychology, to a time when looking bad or of lesser value in front of the rest of the tribe could get us kicked out and leave us on our own to face the saber-toothed tiger and other dangers. Safety in numbers meant we needed to fit in with the group if we wanted to stay alive.

Disrespect is a major source of boundary violation, and in most situations that lead to anger, you'll find an element of disrespect. Thoughtless treatment, criticism, and anything that reflects badly on the self will trigger that ancient part of our brain, and a chain reaction will begin. Feelings of abandonment and rejection will lead to fear for our survival, which we then experience as anger so we can defend ourselves.

When someone or something that you value and identify with does not fulfill your expectations or threatens your sense of ownership, you may respond in a hurtful way. For example, imagine that you tell your brother about an argument with your mother, and he doesn't support your perspective on the quarrel. You will experience discomfort and react accordingly. If your boss chooses not to use an idea that you have invested a great deal of time creating and presenting, the wound to your ego will be extremely unpleasant. These reactions to violations of the ego are simply more subtle variations of the fight-or-flight response. Now, we generally don't retaliate physically to those kinds of offenses, but we might strike back with sarcasm, criticism, and insults. Throwing back in someone's face something that was told to us in confidence is also an effective attempt to reverse the pain, but any one of these attacks is an effort to repair a breached boundary. For example, you might tell your brother what your mother said about his new girlfriend.

While some might lash out as their fight response, others withdraw emotionally—using the flight response. Sulking, the cold shoulder, and withholding affection are all emotional methods of running away, and allow one to restore boundaries. Ultimately, even though the fight-or-flight response is natural and serves a purpose, there are more effective ways of handling the fear-to-anger phenomenon.

If you ignore your anger, however, you're closing your eyes to potential dangers to your physical and emotional well-being. When you feel anger, you are being wounded at some level, probably emotional. It's crucial to stay with your anger long enough to figure out what's going on.

ANGER: IDENTIFYING UNMET NEEDS

Some of the messages that anger delivers have to do with unmet needs. Suppose we could have a chat with Max after his mother rebuffs him and tells him to go play. We might find out that he has quite a list of needs that are going unmet. In this case, his mother and father are doing a good job of meeting his basic physical needs: food, shelter, clothing. But Max is missing out on some basic emotional needs, and they all begin with A.

   Accessibility: Although he's only 10, Max has learned that his
      mother and father are often busy with something else, and
      his presence isn't welcome.
   Attention: Even when he's present, Max sometimes feels like
      they're really not listening—they're just pretending to
      hear what he says.
   Affection: Max loves to go visit his friend Andy's house.
      Andy's mom hugs him more often than his own mother
      does.
   Appreciation: You'd probably have to tell Max what you mean
      by that. He knows there are expectations he has to meet—
      about behavior and appearance and grades in school. He
      doesn't get much feedback, though, when he meets them.
   Acceptance: In the deepest part of our hearts, we all need to
      know we belong within a certain social circle, with family
      or a friend. Like appreciation, acceptance is in short sup-
      ply for Max.

When all of these needs are met, the sum is engagement, the sense that we are connected to the people around us. We can rely on them to be interested in what we say and do, to care about our well-being, and to offer their support. In return, we do the same for them. Whether or not we have a genetic bond with these people, they are family, and we need them.

To begin discovering what needs of yours may not be getting met, or what boundaries may be getting crossed, try the next exercise.

EXERCISE: WHY AM I ANGRY?

1. Think about the last time you got angry.
2. If you're an anger dumper, you probably exhibited the fight part of the response, perhaps shouting or at the least making a cynical remark. If you're an anger with-holder, you may see that you withdrew suddenly, exhibiting the flight response.
3. Once you've recalled the incident, picture the scenario in detail in your mind. Make some notes in your anger journal.
4. Now focus specifically on the triggering event. What was it that set you off? Recall what words, actions, or thoughts preceded your response. Be as specific as you can. Was it something someone said or did? Was it your own performance that brought on the anger? What, in particular, was so offensive to you that it sparked your outrage or sudden withdrawal or shutting down? Was a boundary being threatened or crossed? Were you in need of something that you didn't get? Write the answer in your anger journal.
5. Trace that triggering event to how it affected you. What part of you—what aspect of your sense of self—was harmed, threatened, or disrespected? What needs were

you feeling? Recognizing these links will help you establish healthy boundaries.

6. Once you have pinpointed the root cause of your anger, take a few minutes to write about your findings. Taking a little time to explore your anger can have huge benefits.

GAINING THE WISDOM OF YOUR ANGER

We can't change other people; we can only change ourselves. But once you digest your emotions, you will discover new options for dealing with the difficulties in your life, and you will experience new strength. Studies of emotion-oriented therapy have shown that processing buried feelings works quickly and effectively in bringing about positive change, including alleviating anxiety and depression and helping to prevent self-destructive behavior. This is because our emotions, once we start listening to them, become a roadmap guiding us toward better decisions.

It is possible to redefine the role that anger plays in your life, whether you've been discharging it inappropriately or repressing it. I have written this book to show you that, instead of being a destructive force in your life, anger can become a positive tool for growth, understanding, intimacy, and closeness.

When we understand how anger works, we can release this emotion in a safe and productive way, having absorbed the wisdom that comes from examining our feelings and listening to their message. Resolving anger requires processing our feelings and releasing them. This practice has multiple steps: feeling the sensations in our body, tracking the emotions and memories, reflecting on the distorted thoughts and beliefs, processing the meaning, choosing how we want to act on the anger, and consciously letting the anger go—producing the freedom that comes with its release.

As you can see, this cycle is very different from how we typically respond to our feelings on autopilot. The difference in the results is equally dramatic. Self-knowledge is the road to emotional freedom. Once you become aware of what your choices are, you understand that choice gives you the power to make your life what you want it to be. The more you understand about what you personally do with angry feelings as well as how they tend to occur for you, the more you'll be able to recognize when your anger is on its way and the more time and choice you'll have in deciding what to do with it when it surfaces. When you are conscious and present, you can choose to explore your anger, rather than resorting to the fight-or-flight response that is hardwired into your body.

This doesn't mean that it's easy to change your reaction to anger. You've been reacting in an automatic way for a long, long time. You learned it throughout your childhood and it has become ingrained. It may even feel like it's who you are. But it isn't. You are far more than the sum of your conditioning—the modeling and messages you received in childhood. In fact, you are much more powerful and capable than you realize. You just need a few tools to wake yourself up from the unconscious process of your mind so you can use your will to make new choices as a strong, independent, thinking person living in the present moment—what you were ultimately designed to be. We all have this potential for self-mastery and actualization.

In the next chapter, I explore mindfulness, an approach to life that can help you reveal and release old angers and emotions left over from childhood. Mindfulness is both broader and deeper than anger. Becoming mindful can have a truly revolutionary impact on your life.

ANGER MYTHS

It's not only families that encourage us to deny, hide, or suppress our anger. Society at large spreads anger myths that tell us to keep our fury out of sight. However, if we

examine these myths even a little, it becomes clear that
they are not logical or true.

Myth: Anger is bad. Be nice so that people will like you.
Reality: Actually, mistrust can result when people don't
know where you really stand.

Myth: Feeling angry will bring more harm than benefit.
Reality: Feeling our anger allows us to identify our needs—
communicating what we learn can help us get what we
want.

Myth: Confronting issues is too painful and uncomfortable.
Reality: Avoidance promotes unresolved issues and even
more pain over time.

Myth: If you let yourself become angry, you will lose control and do something you'll regret.
Reality: Anger is more likely to erupt in out-of-control
emotional outbursts if it is regularly suppressed.

Myth: If you let yourself feel your anger, you won't be able
to accomplish the things you need to do.
Reality: It's empowering to be aware of the anger that's in
your body. By experiencing these feelings, you will be able
to determine how you feel about a situation and make
mindful choices about what you want to do.

Myth: Anger is not good for relationships.
Reality: Expressing your anger in mindful, safe, and appropriate ways can actually strengthen your relationships.

CHAPTER 3

Mindfulness as a Strategy

Sometimes your mind feels like a snow globe that has just been shaken. Instead of the blizzard of snowflakes, all sorts of thoughts and flashes of memory buzz through your consciousness—and take you out of the present moment. On a busy day, haven't you been surprised to find yourself arriving at your destination, when actually you set out half an hour ago? Worse yet, you don't remember exactly how you got there. At times like this, tell yourself, "I live in the current moment and make it my home." Close your eyes for a moment and imagine the snowfall slowing gently to a little flurry of flakes. As the last of them settle to the ground, imagine the stillness and beauty at the end of a fresh snowfall. This is the gift that mindfulness can bring to your life.

WHAT IS MINDFULNESS?

Mindfulness is the state of mind in which we intentionally focus on ourselves in the present. In this state, we observe our thoughts and feelings but do not judge them. In addition, we do not concern ourselves with the past or the future. The goal of mindfulness is to live in the present moment without being distracted or preoccupied. Buddhists practice mindfulness as a way to achieve greater consciousness and to break out of automatic living—just going through the motions of the day without being particularly aware of your environment or your reactions to it. As part of mindfulness, they encourage us to be curious and to explore our own nature and reactions.

In essence, mindfulness is about waking up, being aware, and participating consciously in our experiences as they happen. If you're not conscious of what's going on both inside and around you, you miss out on a lot of life's most beautiful gifts. You can also lose sight of how you are contributing to your own problems. This is certainly true regarding how we react to anger and what we do to create it. In this chapter, you'll learn the techniques of mindfulness step by step so that, going forward, you can use this strategy to examine the anger in your life and to achieve emotional freedom.

LEARNING TO BE MINDFUL

If you're reading this book, chances are that the idea of living in mindfulness of the moment may be something relatively new to you. That's okay. We're going to start out with some very simple techniques to introduce you to mindfulness in an easy and fun way.

Meditation on the Breath

Meditation on the breath is fundamental to mindfulness. It helps you focus on the present moment of experience, and that is essential to everything that comes after. A bonus of this exercise is that it will help you calm the mind and quiet any anxiety in your body that may be related to short, shallow breathing. You might impatiently say, "I know how to breathe already." But have you been paying attention?

EXERCISE: MINDFUL BREATHING

1. Find a quiet place where you will be undisturbed for at least 10 minutes. Sit comfortably and close your eyes.

2. Begin by noting how cool air enters the nose, then warm air is exhaled. Don't try to hold your breath, push it out, or change the natural rhythm—rather, just be aware.

3. Counting will help you stay focused on breathing, when distracting thoughts start to intrude. You can count any way you like. Perhaps you'll choose to count "one" as you inhale and "two" as you exhale. If you count "one" as you inhale and "one" as you exhale, then "two" in and "two" out, and so on, up to "five," you'll get a sense of how your body calms over time. But you can simply repeat "one, one, one, one" as you inhale and exhale. Don't force your breath—just follow its natural rhythm.

4. Even though you're focused on breathing, your mind may wander to other thoughts. When this happens, just note the thought and return to counting the breath, beginning with "one."

You may be surprised at how much happens during the simple act of breathing. Take out your anger journal and make note of your experience. This kind of focused breathing is the starting point for all the exercises described in this book. From now on, I'll just say, "Focus your breathing," and you'll know what to do.

Mindfulness of Your Body

Many of us go through the day living in our head: the conversation we had last night, the to-do list for today, the bills that are waiting to be paid next week. Focused this way, we fail to appreciate the most basic aspects of our life: the feel of cloth—or a passing breeze—on our skin, the taste of a chocolate bar, the comfort of a familiar chair.

This exercise introduces you to the concept of mindfulness by asking you to be more conscious of sensations in your body. Only then can you fully feel and release your emotions, the goal of this book. So let's begin by eating mindfully. I've chosen a fruit that offers a great deal of stimulation to awaken the senses—the orange. You'll need an orange and some napkins.

EXERCISE: MINDFULLY EATING AN ORANGE

1. Sit cross-legged on the floor, holding an orange in your cupped hands. Focus your breathing.
2. Rub the outside of your orange, taking in the texture of the rough skin. Feel the weight of the orange as you bounce it gently in your hands.
3. Begin to peel the orange. Pay attention to the scent that is released when the skin of the fruit is punctured, the stickiness of the orange's juices, the way the slices slightly resist being separated.
4. Now place a slice or half a slice of orange in your mouth. How does the piece of orange feel on the tongue? How does it taste when you bite down? Does the second slice taste different from the first? How many slices does it take before you've had enough?
5. Now turn your attention from the orange to your other sensations and emotions. How do you feel? Joyful, frustrated, excited, irritated?
6. Make some notes in your anger journal about the experience.

This awareness exercise can be done with apples or raisins instead of oranges. Or it can be adapted to other simple activities, such as brushing your teeth or taking a shower. In each case, make sure you are paying attention to every aspect of the experience: Do you have an order for brushing your teeth? How does the brush feel against your gums? Pay attention to the taste of the paste you use. Rub your tongue over your teeth before and after you brush. What's the difference?

Mindfulness of Your Environment

Unless we're in a strange place, we often ignore our environment. We know the streets between our house and the neighborhood market. Although our eyes and ears are theoretically open, we can move between the two—walking or driving—with no conscious recollection of the trip. In this exercise, you're going to pay special attention to your location in the world.

EXERCISE: TAKING IN THE ENVIRONMENT

1. Choose a spot that's familiar to you—one you think you know like the back of your hand. You might sit on a bench in a nearby park, for instance, or in your favorite chair or sofa in your living room.
2. Find a place where you can be still for a few minutes— standing, sitting, or lying down. Close your eyes, and focus on your breathing.
3. First, connect with your skin. Are you hot or cold or just right? How do your clothes feel on your body? Is there any movement in the air around you? Is your body comfortable? If an arm or leg is in an awkward position, adjust yourself until you feel at ease.
4. Now, open your nostrils to the world around you. Take in the smells. If you're inside, you might smell dust or old cooking aromas. If you're outside, you might smell

flowers, or grass, or the exhaust of passing cars. Take a moment to sort out all the smells.

5. We're ready for sounds now. If you pay attention, you're likely to find layers of sound in your environment, beginning at your body and progressing into the distance: the breath moving in and out of your lungs, a clock on the wall, a door shutting somewhere down the street, a bird's song. Attend to each of them in turn.

6. Finally, you can open your eyes. You might want to look for the items that have generated the other sensations you were just feeling. Instead of naming the objects, focus on the shapes and colors of whatever surrounds you.

7. When you are finished with this sensory inventory, take out your anger journal and make some notes on what you took in. Don't forget to record how you felt during the exercise. Were you anxious, amused?

Mindfulness of Your Thoughts and Feelings

Mindfulness leads inevitably to meditation, a focused awareness of the thinking process. A lot of people seem to think they can't meditate, but really it just takes relaxation and practice. Here are a couple of exercises that can help. In both cases, you will need to read the exercise in advance, then practice it. Some people find it useful to record their own voice reading the directions. If you do that, allow a pause between steps, so that you have time to engage in the experience. The purpose is to slow down, observe thoughts, and release them or let them go without judgment.

EXERCISE: MEDITATION ON THE BUBBLE

1. Begin by sitting in a comfortable position, with your back straight and shoulders relaxed. Softly close your eyes, and focus on your breathing.
2. Imagine bubbles slowly rising up in front of you. Each bubble contains a thought, feeling, or perception.
3. See the first bubble rise up. What is inside? See the thought, observe it, and watch it slowly float away. Try not to judge, evaluate, or think about it more deeply.
4. Once it has floated out of sight, watch the next bubble appear.
5. What is inside? Observe it, and watch it slowly float away. If your mind goes blank, then watch the bubble rise up with "blank" inside and slowly float away.

Now I'm going to encourage creativity and imagination. It may be an especially helpful kind of meditation if you experience a lot of anxiety.

EXERCISE: VISUALIZATION

1. Begin by sitting in a comfortable position, with your back straight and shoulders relaxed. Softly close your eyes, and focus on your breathing.
2. Allow the picture in your mind to become blank. You are going to imagine a place that feels comfortable, safe, and relaxing. Think of your place. It might be the beach, a lake, or even your own bed. Imagine it slowly appearing before you, becoming more and more clear. We'll call this your safe place.
3. Look to your left. What do you see? Look to your right. What is over there? Look closer.

4. Breathe in. What do you smell? Walk around your place. Look closer at certain things. Stay focused on your place.
5. How are you feeling? If you find your thoughts wandering, observe them, and then focus on bringing the image of your place back into focus in front of you. (Allow some time.)
6. When you are ready, put your hand in front of your eyes. Open your eyes. Slowly spread your fingers to allow light in. When you are ready, slowly remove your hand.

Be sure to take out your anger journal and describe the place you found comfortable, safe, and relaxing. One way to use your anger productively, to find the time to hear its message, is to go to your interior safe place when you are feeling the first sensations of anger. You might want to draw a picture of it or give it a name.

COMMON OBSTACLES IN PRACTICING MINDFULNESS

It can take a while to get used to a mindfulness practice. Following are some typical problems people encounter and ways to overcome them.

You Can't Get Into It

When you first try mindfulness exercises, you may feel blocked, anxious, or resistant to exploring your inner world. You may believe there's nothing going on inside you. If you've never done this type of work before, you might need to make several attempts at mindfulness before any information about your internal activities will surface. The more you work at being mindful, the more readily the experience will come to you. If you just can't get into it, try exploring your lack of response as an inner experience. What does it feel like to be blocked? What comes up when you focus on your feelings of resistance? What does "nothing" feel like? By starting with what's happening in the moment, you can jump-start the mindfulness process.

Roger

I had a patient named Roger who received a message in childhood that he wasn't entitled to his feelings. After working several months to help Roger access his feelings, I tried doing a mindfulness exercise with him. During the exercise, he opened his eyes almost immediately and told me, "I don't feel anything. I don't understand what's supposed to happen."

I replied, "You were never given permission to have your feelings, so they can be scary and feel foreign to you. Try going back inside and experiencing what 'nothing' is like." Roger experienced some agitation but couldn't stay with it. We noticed that his agitation was acting as a defense from accessing his internal emotions.

Over the next several months, I continued to work with Roger to get him present in his body and in touch with his feelings and sensations. Every week we did grounding and sensory awareness exercises and practiced brief mindfulness meditations (similar to the ones you will find in this book). I also reminded him at times not to get discouraged, emphasizing that because he hadn't received permission to have his feelings as a child—and therefore hadn't paid much attention to them growing up—they might take him a while to access. I urged him not to give up.

Fortunately, he persisted. Though it took Roger some time, due to his determination and steadfastness, eventually the mindfulness process worked for him and he was able to be present with his feelings.

You Try to Control Your Experience

Sometimes people think they are perceiving their authentic inner world when they are actually pushing their experience in a certain direction. It's essential to allow your mindfulness practice to flow naturally. The best way to do this is to relax and see what comes up for you. Let go of any judgments or expectations you may have. Make it your goal to observe objectively. You don't have to figure anything out. Just be curious. If you keep your approach neutral, you'll open the doors to honesty—there is no need for shame or defensiveness, for guardedness or withholding the truth. With mindfulness, you get to explore what's really going on—to observe what is.

You Want to Stick with Your Story

If you're using mindfulness in therapy, the desire to hold on to your preconceived notions about where you are in your life can be an issue. In my practice, I see patients who would prefer to talk right over their feelings and continue to tell a version of their lives that keeps them stuck in victimhood. Continuing to tell the negative story only perpetuates it. Focusing on their story also makes it possible for these patients to avoid their feelings. I encourage them to slow down to see what's going on inside of them. Progress may come in fits and starts before they get used to the mindfulness process. And when they start to get to their feelings—as the feelings begin to surface—I work hard to keep them from running for the exit.

BEING MINDFUL ANYTIME, ANYWHERE

Mindfulness may seem to be an activity that must be done in a darkened room with incense burning. But that's not the case. The beauty of this practice is that it's available to you any time of day, no matter where you are or what you're doing.

Whenever you feel the need for greater emotional clarity, or you want to move through difficult thoughts and feelings, go within. Mindfulness can let you discover what's beneath your reaction to a situation, such as anger. Mindfulness can get you in touch with the charge behind your anger—which may come in part from an experience in the past.

Some of the learning exercises in this chapter require special attention to time and space, but the truth is, you can be mindful anytime, anywhere. Here's a basic exercise to use whenever you'd like to practice being more mindful.

EXERCISE: BASIC MINDFULNESS

1. Wherever you find yourself, sit comfortably and focus on your breathing. You may close your eyes if it helps you to achieve an inner quiet more quickly.
2. Switch your attention from thoughts of the past or future to an awareness of the present. If your eyes were closed, open them now.
3. Begin looking around, noticing the sights and sounds of your environment. Observe the details. For instance, perhaps you're sitting in the family room, and you're taking in the sensory details of your surroundings: the color and texture of the curtains, the warmth and smoothness of your favorite mug, the subtle taste of your coffee or tea, the soft cushioning of your sofa or chair. Or maybe you're in a car, waiting for the traffic

to begin moving again. Feel the strength of your hands on the wheel; look at the sky—what's the weather brewing?

4. If any thoughts that are not about the present try to emerge, just say "wandering" and go back to breathing. Acknowledge any thought but don't engage with it; just let it pass, and then shift your focus back to the current environment.

5. Joyfully take in all of the details of the moment. Remember to breathe and relax.

6. After a few minutes, move on with your day.

Because this exercise is simple and easy to do, you can stop a few times each day for a mindfulness break. You can also incorporate mindfulness practice into your day more casually. Go about your activities more slowly, focusing on your experience of each one. This means no multitasking. I can't emphasize enough just how important it is to slow down—move slowly, speak slowly, pay attention to what you're doing now. Doing so will help you become more and more conscious of your experience in the present.

You'll be surprised at the impact that taking a few quiet, mindful moments can have on your life. It helps you to be fully present for the next interaction with your child or to be centered for a discussion with your partner, parent, coworker, or boss. Being mindful can help you experience each moment with fewer mental filters, so you are not seeing life through the lens of your past experiences or against the backdrop of the day's to-do list. This is not a time to figure anything out, just a time to be in the moment.

A note about safety: Sometimes you'll want to maintain a dual (inner and outer) awareness when being mindful. When you're driving, for example, you might want to observe your inner experience and the passing scene, but you'll also want to keep your eyes on the road to avoid an accident. If you're watching your kids, you'll need to be present with what's going on outside you even if you are focusing within.

MINDFULNESS IS OUR RESPONSIBILITY

I hope that by now I've persuaded you that mindfulness is a strategy you can use. Now I'm going to take you a step further: Mindfulness is a strategy you should use. We can choose to seek awareness. We have the power and the free will to control how conscious or unconscious we are. In a particular circumstance, we can opt to pay full attention, no attention at all, or some level of attention in between. In other words, we can be mindful, mindless, or some combination of the two. According to our choice, we can grasp the truth of a situation—or we can remain oblivious to it.

To take responsibility for yourself and your anger, the first step is to become conscious of your own behavior—including what's going on inside. It's our responsibility to be mindful of what we're doing and what's going on inside of us, including our own feelings of anger.

You may not realize that you've been moving mindlessly through life—it can be a habit, as we say, to go through the motions. You might wonder how it is possible to become mindful. Here is the key: In the moments when you are aware, consciously make it your intention to be aware all the time. Accept this as your responsibility, and make it your mission. In this way, over time, you will train yourself to be mindful.

In the beginning, you can also make notes for yourself as reminders to pay attention. Use sticky notes where you might most need to be mindful: in your car, on your vanity mirror, next to your computer, on your smartphone, in your wallet. The message can be simple: "Be here now." You can also take the opportunity offered by quiet moments to ask yourself, "What's going on with me now? What do I feel at this moment?"

Everyone has the innate ability to be mindful—and to reap the benefits of self-awareness. It's your choice: Do you want to view yourself and your environment more clearly and completely? Doing so will let you handle life's challenges more effectively—and enjoy a richer appreciation of life's beauties.

CHAPTER 4

How Anger Feels

Anger is a powerful emotion that feels uncomfortable as it moves through the body. When our anger is triggered, many physical changes occur inside us. Our breathing deepens and quickens. Our heart beats faster, too, and it can feel like it's racing. Blood vessels constrict, and muscles tighten. Basically, what we're experiencing is the famous fight-or-flight response: Sensing a threat, we are preparing either to do battle or to run away as fast as we can. The intensity of our sensations creates tremendous tension within us, and we may feel a powerful impulse to lash out verbally or physically to get relief from our discomfort.

In this age of psychotherapy, however, fresher approaches to this discomfort—ways to circumvent our anger—are being proposed. Many people seek counseling for unresolved anger, and patients I saw early in my therapy career were using all of the popular communication methods to deal with anger—"I statements" (e.g., "I feel angry when . . ." and "What I hear you saying is . . .") and role-playing among them. These strategies may have offered some temporary relief, and it might have taken some pressure off their relationships, but I couldn't help but notice that their anger wasn't going away. I could see in their taut faces, harsh voices, and tight body language that their bodies were still hanging on to it. I soon came to realize that these patients could talk about their anger until they were blue in the face and it wouldn't be enough. Not only did they need to understand their anger intellectually; they needed to fully feel it. But, initially, most were too afraid to go there.

ANGER IS UNCOMFORTABLE

What were my clients afraid of? Basically, it was the discomfort created by their angry feelings and what those feelings might reveal. The addictions that have become so prevalent around the world—drugs and alcohol, sex, shopping, workaholism— prove that people will do anything and everything to avoid feelings. Some people are even afraid of being alone because it brings up too many feelings. I once had a patient in his 40s who talked to himself so he could avoid the thoughts he might have when he was alone. He had started the habit as a young boy because he was left by himself so much of the time. As an adult, he arranged his whole life so that he could avoid his feelings, including anger, because they were so painful.

Most of us find anger uncomfortable on several levels. Besides experiencing the physical sensations that arise when we ourselves are angry, we're also uncomfortable about what it might mean when others are angry with us. Each of us is highly sensitive to potential anger—other people's anger as well as our own. Let's say you've been having a meeting with your business partner when she abruptly walks out, goes to her own office, and makes an angry phone call. Despite the absence of any evidence, you may assume she is angry at you. Or say you arrive quite late to your friend's birthday party; because you feel guilty and fear her anger, you avoid apologizing, and then you wonder why she seems to be avoiding you. Even a casual collision with another person on a city sidewalk might put you on your guard against repercussions. And if someone does get angry at you, you might lie, cheat, or worse to alleviate your discomfort and diffuse the threat.

Our own anger, too, can be frightening. Feeling intense anger at a fellow driver might make you worry that you'll be distracted or put yourself in danger. Sometimes the rage we feel at our own children can be deeply upsetting and guilt provoking. Worst of all, we're uncomfortable sitting with our feelings—setting aside distractions and examining our sensations and emotions—to find out what they might reveal.

What's so counterintuitive about the discomfort anger causes is that it was designed that way. That's how anger does the job it was created to do. Anger is one of our emotions, and emotions play an important role in our lives by providing us with information about ourselves and our environment. The goal is to be able to fully experience our emotions, particularly the various shades of anger, in our body as they're happening so that they don't get buried and so that we get the valuable information they hold for us. To be able to do that—to be able to feel our emotions fully— we must learn how to experience discomfort. It's healthy to allow yourself to be emotionally uncomfortable once in a while. Without discomfort, there is no change and no growth. In this chapter, we're going to learn how to use the strategies of mindfulness to get in touch with our sensations and our emotions, especially those related to anger, so that we can receive the important messages that anger and other emotions are trying to deliver.

USING MINDFULNESS TO GET IN TOUCH WITH YOUR INNER WORLD

When I teach mindfulness as a psychological tool, I present it as a way for my patients to purposely slow down in order to gain a deeper awareness of their internal self—including their sensations, emotions, impulses, thoughts, and memories. Patients learn to take time to make sure they aren't distracted by the external world, so they can be mindful of their internal experience. In this valuable self-discovery, emotional healing begins.

This kind of mindfulness, which focuses specifically on what is happening in our inner world, is called emotional mindfulness. As it relates to anger, emotional mindfulness is tremendously helpful because it can make you more aware of your impulse to vent or suppress anger. Being emotionally aware also gives you insight into the causes of your upset—and your options for responding to it.

Emotional mindfulness lets us experience and address the emotions we feel in our body as they are happening. It might seem counterintuitive to try to get up close and personal with painful feelings, when the logical reaction is to run from them. We're geared to avoid pain and seek pleasure. But change requires discomfort, and experiencing our feelings helps us get what we want in life—good health, freedom from addiction, and so on. The key to healing is feeling our feelings.

We can categorize sensations and emotions into two general groups—comfortable and uncomfortable. While our personal history has an impact on our feelings, we must also look for the cause of our feelings in what's happening right now. That means paying attention to the messages from our body. The good thing about listening to the body is that it never lies (unlike the mind, which covers up a lot). The emotions we feel in our body will help us understand what we think and believe, as well as what we need. By accepting this fundamental truth, you'll be able to care for your emotional health. You will have the ability to reduce emotional discomfort by first recognizing the pain, then ending it by giving yourself exactly what you need or want.

The Body Doesn't Lie

To improve our emotional lives and our relationships, we need to know what is going on inside us. Our bodies register all of our experiences, including instances of anger, fear, and sad-

ness; physical injuries; invasive medical procedures; and acci-
dents. These episodes can traumatize and debilitate us. Ideally,
we recognize, process, and release the difficult emotions caused
by ordeals such as these. On the other hand, suppressing painful feelings can impede the flow of energy in the body, which
can weaken the immune system and lead to illness and other
issues. To correct this internal imbalance, we must process and
release our denied emotions—finally facing the truth of our
experience.

If you aren't convinced that your interactions with the world
affect how your body works, consider the phenomenon of neuroplasticity—the brain's natural ability to restructure itself by
forming new pathways of neurons. There are two types of neuroplasticity: the type that occurs as the normal brain matures
through adulthood and the type that occurs in response to
injury or environmental changes.

A friend of mine suffered the trauma of sudden hearing loss—total deafness, temporary or permanent, with an
unknown cause. When she sat down to lunch with friends, her
left ear was uncomfortable—as if she had just gotten off a plane
and her ear hadn't yet cleared. By the time she got up to leave,
she couldn't hear a thing out of that ear. Driving home, she
could see that the oncoming traffic was passing to her left, but
from the sound of it, all those cars were rushing by on the passenger side—only her right ear was working. Within a couple
of days, her brain had adapted, so she heard the traffic passing
to her left, even though that ear remained totally deaf. This was
just the first of a series of maneuvers her brain made to help
her cope with the ongoing loss.

The same type of adaptive neuroplasticity occurs in all areas
of our being and continues throughout a lifetime, informed
by our actions and surroundings. For example, science has
shown that when we purposely focus our attention—which is
what happens when we practice mindfulness—new neuronal

connections form in the brain allowing us to literally change our minds, adapt new thought processes, and grow.

Embracing the truth of our experiences, including anger, is crucial for our mental and physical well-being. Recognizing our true feelings makes it possible for us to change behaviors and situations that do not support us—leading to a more honest, satisfying life. The way to begin resolving poor anger styles is to feel our anger. This takes emotional mindfulness.

Emotional Mindfulness Is Body Oriented

Many mindfulness techniques are body oriented, meaning they explore what your body can tell you about your life. They provide a way to tap into your rich inner sphere—your impulses, feelings, thoughts, and beliefs. Mindfulness allows you to observe nonjudgmentally what is happening from moment to moment. By not judging, you are more likely to see things clearly.

With time and with mindfulness practice, you'll get more and more in touch with the internal information that is available to you.

Internal Activities

Body sensations
Emotions
Thoughts
Beliefs
Impulses
Memories
Worries
Judgments
Moods

Mental images
Muscle tightness (body tension)
Strategies

SENSATIONS: THE LANGUAGE OF THE BODY

Focusing attention on the sensory experiences of your body will bring you fully into yourself in the present moment, a crucial element of mindfulness. This is an important first step to get in touch with the emotional and mental levels of your being.

Sensation is the perception of stimuli through the senses (sight, hearing, smell, taste, and touch). Sensation also refers to the physical feeling that results when the senses are stimulated (e.g., warmth) or when there is a change inside the body (e.g., cramping). In some cases, a sensation may be a general feeling with no directly attributable stimulus (e.g., discomfort).

Your body speaks to you through sensations. Physical feelings are essentially the words your body uses to communicate with you. Based on the previous examples, your sensations might tell you, "I'm warm," "I'm cramping," or "I'm uncomfortable." Some messages may be loud ("That burns!"); others may be quiet ("I'm relaxed") or may even pass unnoticed.

The gift of sensations is that they can put us in touch with our immediate needs—and with emotions, including anger, that may otherwise go unrecognized. In many cases, we must choose to hear our body's messages. This is where mindfulness comes in. Being mindful of sensations is a self-compassionate way to get vital information about our internal activities. With this information, we can begin to make positive changes in our behavior.

Be careful not to mix up sensations and emotions. There is a fine distinction. Think of sensations as physical feelings and responses, and emotions as states of consciousness. Sensations may accompany emotions, but they are not the same thing. For example, consider the emotion of anger. For some, anger might be associated with the sensations of trembling, a racing heart, butterflies in the stomach, and throbbing temples. As another example, cringing is a sensation; disgust is an emotion. Breathlessness is a sensation; excitement is an emotion. Blushing is a sensation; embarrassment is an emotion.

Following is a partial list of sensations and words that describe sensations. Can you think of additional examples?

Sensations and Words That Describe Sensations

Beating	Dry	Heavy
Blushing	Dull	Hollow
Breathless	Effervescent	Hot
Bruised	Empty	Hungry
Burning	Enlarged	Immobile
Chilly	Exhausted	Increased
Clammy	Expanding	Inflamed
Clenched	Expansive	Inflated
Closed	Faint	Invigorated
Cold	Fast	Itchy
Confused	Fatigued	Knotted
Cool	Floating	Lifeless
Cramping	Flooding	Light
Crushing	Flowing	Limp
Damp	Fluttery	Nauseated
Decreased	Freezing	Numb
Dissociated	Full	Obstructed
Distorted	Goose bumps	Open
Dizzy	Hard	Painful

Pins and needles	Smothering	Tense
Pounding	Soft	Thick
Pressure	Sore	Throbbing
Pulsating	Spasm	Tickling
Quivering	Spinning	Tight
Relaxed	Squeezed	Tingling
Released	Stabbing	Trembling
Scratchy	Stiff	Twisted
Sensitive	Still	Twitching
Serene	Stimulated	Unsteady
Shaky	Stinging	Vibrating
Sharp	Sweaty	Warm
Shuddering	Swollen	Weak
Skittish	Taut	Wet
Slow	Tender	

Now that you have looked over the list, I'd like you to experience what we're talking about. This brief exercise will give you the chance to become aware of some of the subtle and perhaps not so subtle sensations that your body is using to speak to you.

EXERCISE: OBSERVING BODY SENSATIONS

1. Find a quiet place where you can sit undisturbed, and focus on your breathing.
2. Now, take few minutes to make a mental inventory of your body. Stop at the location in your body where you typically hold everyday tension. Do not choose a place in your body that has been injured recently or that is very painful.
3. Focus on your selected body part. Observe the main sensation around it. If you aren't quite sure which word best describes the sensation you are experiencing, refer to the

list above. For example, do you feel pressure in your head? Pain in your neck? Knots in your stomach? Or do you perceive a pleasant sensation, such as relaxation in your back? Write down what you sense in your anger journal.

4. For about 5 minutes, continue observing this focal point in your body. Do not attempt to improve or modify what you are feeling. Does the sensation remain constant? Or does your attention somehow alter it? If the sensation transforms into something else, what word from the list identifies it? Write down what you sense.

5. Now think of the last time you were angry. Try to remember the incident in detail: Who was with you? What was said? How did you respond?

6. Do another inventory of your body. Are you experiencing sensations in new places? These may well be the sensations associated with anger.

In the exercise, did you have any trouble naming your sensations? Don't be disappointed if you are unable to perceive and describe your sensations at first. Tuning in to your internal activities takes practice, like any skill. Repeat the Observing Body Sensations exercise when you have time. If you can't spare 5 minutes, take just a moment to check in with the feelings in your body. Try to identify each sensation in one word.

Over time, you will become able to easily recognize and communicate what your body is experiencing. Paying attention to your sensations in this way lets you begin to get in touch with your real experience.

EMOTIONS: MESSENGERS FROM YOUR HEART

Once you've been able to identify a sensation in your body, the next step is to figure out what that sensation is telling you about your real experience. One way to gain this understanding is to uncover and explore the emotions associated with the sensation. This process will help you reconnect with your feelings, including anger.

Ruby

Ruby, 26, sat in my office, telling me about all the ways her boyfriend treated her badly. When she finished her story, she said, "You can see how much I put up with." The revealing part was that she was laughing the whole time she told me the story about her abuse. And, believe me, it was anything but funny. I was flabbergasted at her denial of what was actually happening to her.

I pointed out her behavior to her, and we talked a little more about it. Then I asked her to take some deep breaths and try to notice what was going on in her body, where her real feelings about her situation could be found. When she said, "Bill abusively stood over me . . ." I stopped her and asked how she experienced saying that to me—what feelings, images, or memories that brought up in her. Each time she stopped mindfully tracking how she was feeling in her body, I interrupted her and suggested we go back to tracking her feelings.

How did I know when Ruby was in her body versus out of it? I track patients' body language, their behaviors, and their words—certain words will get us internally focused on our experience. Otherwise, patients will just talk over the experience rather than feeling it. People go slower when they're being mindful and reflective. If we're not present, we won't be able to feel our real feelings or know our real experience. When I use the word *present*, I mean that a person is fully in his or her body. We have a tendency to separate from our body in certain circumstances; for example, when we are afraid, agitated, or confused. In these cases, we feel that the world is unsafe, so we retreat from it. When we abandon ourselves in this way, dissociating from our uncomfortable feelings, we leave ourselves vulnerable—because we are no longer in our body to protect ourselves. As you can see by this example, when we're out of touch with our real experience—how we really feel—we often let others victimize us. If we are to remain present during challenging situations, we must realize that it is safe to stay in our body, in touch with our feelings. In fact, this is the only position from which we can live fully and be true to ourselves.

A helpful tool for becoming fully present is noticing and naming your sensations and emotions. In the last exercise, you learned to assign words to your sensations. Let's do the same thing with emotions. Recognizing the sometimes subtle distinctions between emotions will give you a greater sense of your experience and a richer knowledge of yourself. It can also help you have more empathy for others, as you better understand what they are experiencing. As with sensations, the language of emotions is a new one that you are learning to interpret and speak.

Exploring the Range of Emotions

Some emotions are more comfortable to experience than others. For example, most, if not all people find joy and love to be pleasant feelings. Anger, fear, and sadness, on the other hand, are experienced as unpleasant. As you read through the following lists of words describing comfortable and uncomfortable emotions, see if you can recall having felt any of them. If so, try to get a sense internally of the specific experience each emotion created in your body.

A Vocabulary for Comfortable Emotions

HAPPINESS/JOY

Blissful	Euphoric	Optimistic
Bubbly	Excited	Peaceful
Buoyant	Festive	Playful
Carefree	Giddy	Pleased
Cheerful	Glad	Satisfied
Content	Inspired	Silly
Delighted	Jolly	Thrilled
Ecstatic	Jubilant	Upbeat
Elated	Lighthearted	
Enthusiastic	Merry	

ENTHUSIASM

Alive	Earnest	Intent
Ardent	Encouraged	Keen
Avid	Excited	Motivated
Breathless	Fervent	Powered up
Dynamic	Gung ho	Spirited
Eager	Hopeful	Zealous

LOVE

Adoring	Enchanted	Seductive
Affectionate	Fond	Sensual
Amorous	Forgiving	Sentimental
Caring	Grateful	Sexy
Cherishing	Infatuated	Soft
Compassionate	Kindly	Sympathetic
Doting	Open	Tender
Empathetic	Passionate	Treasuring
Enamored	Romantic	Warm

A Vocabulary for Uncomfortable Emotions

ANGER

Agitated	Fuming	Livid
Aggravated	Furious	Mad
Annoyed	Grumpy	Mean
Belligerent	Hateful	Miffed
Bitter	Heated	Offended
Boiling	Ill-tempered	Pissed off
Brooding	Incensed	Resentful
Contemptuous	Indignant	Riled
Cross	Inflamed	Upset
Disgusted	Infuriated	Vengeful
Displeased	Irascible	Wrathful
Enraged	Irate	
Frustrated	Irritated	

HURT

Aching	Distressed	Torn
Battered	Injured	Tortured
Bruised	Pained	Wounded
Crushed	Shamed	
Devastated	Suffering	

SADNESS

Crestfallen	Dismal	Heartbroken
Defeated	Down	Heavy hearted
Dejected	Dreadful	Helpless
Depressed	Dreary	Hollow
Despairing	Dull	Hopeless
Despondent	Forlorn	Impotent
Disappointed	Gloomy	In the dumps
Discouraged	Glum	Inconsolable

Melancholy	Out of sorts	Unhappy
Miserable	Passive	Useless
Moody	Powerless	Weepy
Morose	Somber	Woeful
Mournful	Sorrowful	Worthless

CONFUSION

Ambivalent	Disoriented	Puzzled
Baffled	Distracted	Spacey
Bemused	Indecisive	Wavering
Bewildered	Lost	Wishy-washy
Dazed	Mixed up	
Disconcerted	Perplexed	

FEAR

Afraid	Horrified	Shaky
Alarmed	Hysterical	Shocked
Anxious	Intimidated	Startled
Daunted	Nervous	Surprised
Desperate	Panicked	Terrified
Fearful	Paralyzed	Threatened
Fidgety	Petrified	
Frightened	Scared	

WORRY

Alert	Hesitant	Suspicious
Antsy	Ill at ease	Tense
Anxious	Insecure	Uneasy
Apprehensive	Nervous	Uncertain
Distrustful	Questioning	Uptight
Doubtful	Skeptical	

Just the reading of these lists acknowledges the enormous variety of emotions most of us feel—and if you're not feeling them, then it's doubly important to get back in touch with them. Here's an exercise that may help.

EXERCISE: FINDING THE FEELINGS LINKED TO YOUR ANGER

1. Find a quiet place, and focus on your breathing.
2. To feel your feelings, you have to be in your body. That's what grounding or centering does for you. Stand with your feet a small distance apart, lining them up with your hips. Notice the support of the floor or ground underneath you. Dig your feet and toes into it. Relax, bend your knees slightly, and allow the surface to carry all of your weight. Really feel how the surface supports you.
3. As you stand, pull your shoulders back. Slowly take several breaths in and out. With your hands, knead the skin on your arms, neck, and shoulders. Focus on the sensations in your body.
4. Recall an anger-triggering incident. Picture the details of the event until you feel the anger rise within you. Say, "I am angry." Practice saying this in different ways—louder, softer, faster, slower.
5. Notice what happens in your body when you practice this way. Name the sensations.
6. Now check for feelings besides anger, if any come up. Name those feelings out loud, one at a time, and own them in the same way ("I am hurt," "I feel embarrassed," and so on).
7. Once you have stated all of the feelings you're aware of, relax your stance. Take a few more deep breaths.

8. Now write about this experience in your anger journal. You might start with the sentences, "It's safe to be present in my body. It's safe to feel my feelings." You can also write about how it feels to jot down that affirmation.

Doing this exercise will give you a lot of information. For one, you'll learn about how you feel regarding owning and expressing your anger. The exercise can be applied to tapping into any feeling, from the more uncomfortable emotions (e.g., anger, worry) to the more comfortable ones (e.g., love, happiness).

For now, however, we're going to stay with anger. In this chapter, you have developed the tools that will allow you to experience your anger more fully, so that you can examine its message before you decide how to respond.

CHAPTER 5

How to Catch Anger in the Act

You may be familiar with the popular anger management techniques ("Count to ten. Pound a pillow. Go in your car and scream"). I hope you can begin to see why this method of handling anger won't help us to actually resolve the problems anger tries to bring to our attention. The purpose of anger management—to try to control or contain our angry behavior—is not enough to actually heal. Anger does not need to be contained; it needs to be processed and digested. Otherwise, it will keep recycling and resurfacing.

So I don't want to help you manage (in other words, shut down) your anger. I want to help you explore it. I don't want you to dump it or deny it—I want you to deal with it, meaning to mindfully observe your anger, listening to its message and learning what this part of yourself is trying to teach you about changes you need to make. To do that, you must slow down once your anger is triggered, so that you won't react to it by discharging or suppressing it. For this task, we need more aptly named impulse control techniques.

In Chapter 4, we learned how mindfulness can put us in touch with our sensations and emotions. Now we're going to apply what we've learned to the moments when our anger is triggered. This provides you with your first alternative to simply resorting to the reflex reaction that you've been so accustomed to using, whether it's dumping or withholding. Instead of continuing to act out anger as if you were emotionally hijacked—or stuffing the anger deep inside—you will learn the first steps to taking back emotional control and doing something productive with your anger—getting to the root of it and hearing what it has to say.

FINDING OUT WHAT PROVOKES YOU

As we saw in Chapter 2, anger is designed to keep us safe, to send us the message that something is wrong and give us the extra power we need to face the presenting challenge—fight or flight. This additional power allows us to drive the perceived threat back and create enough distance between us and the danger that we can feel safe. We know that anger can be triggered when we feel a threat to our boundaries, an affront or insult. The varying intensity of our angry response—from annoyance and irritation all the way to fury and rage—determines how offensive a situation seems to us and what level of protection we feel we need. Our anger may also be a response when our basic emotional needs are not met by significant others in our life. The situations that invoke our anger are often called triggers or hot buttons. Some common triggers are:

- Situations that we feel are unfair or unjust
- Actions that cause us to feel disrespected, hurt, frustrated, or disappointed
- Things we simply don't like, such as irritations and annoyances

Once we know what kinds of things set off our anger, we can stop ourselves from pulling the trigger and firing the gun. We can choose more consciously how we want to respond. The following exercise will get you started in mindfully identifying your own anger triggers.

EXERCISE: WHAT MAKES ME ANGRY

1. Find a quiet place to sit and focus your breathing.
2. Open your anger journal, and answer the following questions:
   - When do I feel the hottest anger?
   - What is it about anger that makes me feel afraid?
   - What makes me sad?
   - When do I just want to be alone?
   - What can someone say or do to drive me crazy?
   - When I'm talking with people, how far do I like them to be away from me? Am I comfortable in crowded parties? Do I prefer to be an arm's length or more from the people I'm talking with?
   - Am I getting the respect that everyone deserves? Why do I feel this way?
   - Do I lose control at times? What's going on when that happens? Is it something someone says?
   - What's going on when I explode or run away?
   - What is my secret weakness?
3. Take some time to go over your answers. If you're an anger dumper, can you identify some of the triggers that make you explode? If you're an anger withholder, can you see what makes you afraid and withdrawn?

There's a great deal of meat in the exercise you just completed. Over the next few days, you may want to return to it frequently.

In particular, if you have new experiences with anger, return to your journal and see if the answers you put there help you understand what occurred.

CATCHING THE IMPULSE THAT PRECEDES YOUR ANGER

The next step is to take your self-discovery a little deeper, becoming mindful of the impulse that precedes the fight-or-flight reaction of your particular anger style. Although many people are not aware of it, there is always an impulse—a sensation that rises up through the body—that precedes any angry reaction. A lot of people confuse this sensation with anger itself, but the two are different. Anger follows the impulse, in much the same way that fireworks rise into the sky then suddenly burst into colorful flames (although not all anger is this dramatic). With anger, mindfulness can help us identify the noticeable clues that alert us that anger is coming, giving us time to make a deliberate choice about how we want to respond. When you catch yourself in the act of getting angry at an early enough point, you can prevent the emotional hijacking that was about to take place and instead behave in a different way. Recognizing that your anger is on the way before you act on it is very empowering. It puts you back in the driver's seat with your anger.

Anger is like a fire that will get out of control if clues aren't discovered, even just one clue. In fact, several clues may be happening simultaneously to indicate that your anger is on the way, and mindfulness can help you uncover them.

Clues That You're Getting Ready to Dump Anger

Physical: Rapid heartbeat, tightness or heaviness in the chest, feeling hot, tension in your neck

Behavioral: Pacing, clenching the fists, raising your voice and changing its tone, staring, tapping or stomping your foot

Emotional: Fear, hurt, jealousy, disrespect, feeling threatened

Mental: Hostile self-talk, fantasies of revenge or aggression, obsessive arguments with others with constant rumination over the issue

Clues That You're Hiding Your Anger

Physical: Feeling more tired than normal, waking up tired, difficulty in getting to sleep or sleeping much more than usual (maybe 12 to 14 hours a day), body stiffness, facial tics, stomach ulcers, headaches

Behavioral: Habitual lateness, procrastination in the completion of imposed tasks, sarcasm, stonewalling, gossiping, excessive politeness, constant cheerfulness, sighing, monotone voice, moving slowly, clenching the jaws, repeated physical movements like leg swinging

Emotional: Irritability, boredom, passivity, apathy, loss of interest

Mental: Cynical or ironic perspective on life, disturbing or frightening dreams, mental fog, depression, bitterness, checking out

The following exercise will help you discover which of your personal anger clues is the most noticeable and reliable in signaling to you that you're about to be mad.

EXERCISE: WHAT IS MY PRIMARY ANGER CLUE?

1. Find a quiet place, and focus your breathing.
2. Read the anger clues again slowly. I suggest reading

through all of them, regardless of your particular anger style.

3. Next, call to mind an angering event and review the details of what happened. See if you can recall how you knew you were angry, or scan your body and thoughts to see if merely recalling the event is generating a clue to your anger. Is your jaw clenching? Did you have thoughts of retaliation or revenge? Did you immediately resort to blaming someone else?

4. Write the clue or clues you are noticing in your anger journal.

5. Go back through Steps 2 to 4 with a few more angering events. Continue to write down the clues you discover.

6. Now observe yourself in real life over the next week. Pay close attention to what's happening inside you as you go through the day. Each evening, take some time with your anger journal to identify the clues you uncovered.

As you experience the heightened awareness and focus that mindfulness brings to your inner world, it will become easy to identify the primary clues that precede your anger. Your primary anger clue is a cornerstone in the process of taking charge of your anger and choosing to explore it rather than react to it.

CONTROLLING THE IMPULSE

The beauty of controlling the impulse that precedes your anger—of stopping yourself short of discharging or burying your anger—is that it gives you the opportunity to explore your anger and reap the rewards it has to offer you. It also gives you a choice of how to respond to your anger. Having looked at the many devastating consequences of acting out our rage, we can see that this is no small benefit. It can turn an out-of-control life into one that is productive, fulfilling, and ripe with meaningful and loving relationships.

So how do we do it? Anger is an emotional energy that resides in our body-mind until it runs its course. It is rich with intelligence—insight and information. Catching the internal signal or clue that anger is on the way makes it possible for us to switch to a mind-set of curiosity and self-investigation about what our anger might have to teach us. This is the gift of mindfulness.

If you blow your top or burn off your adrenaline without examining your anger, you won't learn the truth that your anger hopes to reveal. The anger management strategies of pounding a pillow and screaming in your car are forms of discharge, and that's not what we want to do. Discharging the feelings before we explore them also throws away the wisdom we might gain from the information they carry. We always have the option, whether we realize it or not, to stop and explore the anger, learn from it and release it, rather than react to it in the same old destructive way that never gives us what we want and only releases the temporary overflow of emotion until the next time our hot buttons get pushed.

Impulse Control Techniques

Now that mindfulness has armed you with a new awareness of the kinds of things that trigger your anger and the impulse that precedes it, start to observe yourself throughout the day. Make it a new personal challenge to catch yourself whenever you notice that you're starting to get angry. Being mindful in this way gives you the key to power—it's a giant step toward a better life because it opens a window of clarity and offers you the gift of choice. When it does, you'll want to be ready and waiting to slow yourself down, so that you won't have to discharge your feelings or withdraw from them. Following are a few suggested impulse control techniques for each of the two major anger styles. Try one of these to control the impulse preceding the anger when you next recognize it.

Dumpers: The goal is to calm yourself down and keep the charge in your body rather than dumping it. Give yourself a time-out, taking several slow, deep breaths, in through the nose and out through the mouth. Count to 10 (or 20 if you need to). Close your eyes and just breathe, telling yourself to relax and not react, that it's okay to sit with the feelings. If you have visualized a safe place to retreat, go there now.

Withholders: The goal for you is to stay present in your body and not run away. Do this by grounding yourself, beginning with the simple containment exercise of hugging yourself tight, really feeling that you're there. You may also try another grounding exercise where, sitting or standing, you grip your toes into the floor, open and close your fists, then grab the opposite forearm in each hand and knead your skin. Keeping your eyes open, focus on staying in your body.

For dumpers and withholders alike, it's important to be in your body—in order to know what you're feeling. Our bodies never lie to us. They only reveal our hidden truth. Our heads, on the other hand, will lead us astray countless times. The exercises in Chapter 4 helped you learn to listen to what's going on inside, and we're continuing that work here. Think about the things that make you angry. It's not what happens to you, but what you think about what happens that determines how you feel. Let's look again at the story of Keith and Stacey—you'll recall that Keith was hoping for a quiet afternoon watching movies on the couch with Stacey, and she insisted on attending a home association mixer—this time seeing it from Stacey's side.

Stacey and Keith

Stacey kept an eye on the driveway as she got dressed for the home association mixer. Keith always took so much time to do the weekend errands. Instead of just going down the list she had prepared for him, he would go wandering off into wine shops and bookstores. She was sure she had reminded him about the home association mixer this morning, but still, he was late. While he was gone, she'd gotten the boys ready for their friend's birthday party, wrapped the gifts, delivered them to the party, cleaned up the house, taken a shower, and gotten dressed.

Finally, she heard the garage door open and close. "Keith, the home association mixer starts in half an hour," she announced as he trudged into the kitchen. "You have just enough time to take a shower and change."

"Oh, I forgot," Keith said, owning up to it. "Listen, I'm really beat. You know how hard I've been working. Let's skip it and hang out at home this afternoon, okay?"

Stacey stared at her husband for a long moment. "No way," she finally responded in a scolding tone. "If you're not going, you're staying here alone. Got it?"

She felt tired, too, but she was determined to go to the mixer. Keith and Stacey and their family had moved to this neighborhood just a few months ago, and she was having a hard time making friends. Stacey worked from home, and she needed some nearby friends to take a walk with or share a coffee—something to provide a social break in the day. She was hoping that she might make some new connections at the mixer.

She sighed as she saw the look on Keith's face as he headed into the living room. It was easy for him—he had lots of friends at work, and he belonged to a Sunday golf club, too. Couldn't he see that she needed someone beyond the family?

Both Keith and Stacey ignored the anger clues—his hostile self-talk, her scolding tone of voice—that might have opened an opportunity to discuss their partnership. Exploring their anger through mindfulness could have made their relationship closer and more rewarding for both of them.

THE ANGER JOURNAL

The anger journal is an extremely useful and valuable self-discovery tool that can help you succeed where Stacey and Keith missed their chance. So far we've been using the anger journal to keep a record of your exercises in self-discovery. You can use the anger journal each time your anger gets provoked, and over time, you will stop overlooking valuable anger clues and get to the heart of the message anger is trying to send you. Each time your anger gets provoked, rather than discharging your feelings or withdrawing from them, sit down with a pen and work through the questions in your anger journal. Here's a very simple outline for writing about an anger incident.

EXERCISE: ANGER ENTRY

1. The anger incident: Describe the angering incident in as much detail as possible. Where were you? What was the time of day? Were you alone or with others? What were you doing or saying just before you began to feel the warning signs of anger?
2. Using the techniques of mindfulness, consider what you were feeling at the moment you got angry. On a scale of 1 to 10, with 1 being mildest and 10 being strongest, how strong was your anger?
3. Which of the following words best describes your anger?
    Annoyance
    Irritation

Exasperation
Resentment
Frustration
Righteousness
Anger
Fury
Rage
Other: _____

4. Anger style: What did you do when you became angry?
    Suppressed (kept to myself)
    Vented outwardly by screaming, yelling, swearing,
        or making sarcastic remarks
    Released by talking it over with a confidant
        (spouse, friend, etc.)
    Released through vigorous exercise or physical
        activities
    Released by throwing or breaking things
    Released through a nasty note or memo
    Expressed through pouting or sulking
    Expressed in a healthy, assertive (rather than
        harmful, aggressive) manner to the person who
        provoked it
    Other: _____
    Write everything you felt in your journal.

5. Anger clues: Write down the anger clues you felt before
    your response. Mindfulness can help you explore your
    physical sensations. Here are some suggestions.
        A tight, knotted feeling in the stomach
        A headache
        A stiff neck
        A clenched jaw
        A pounding heart
        Clenched fists
        Faster breathing

Lump in the throat
Shakiness
Eating and more eating
Smoking
Drinking
Taking drugs
Ruminating over the other person or the issue
Retaliatory or vengeful thoughts
Other: _____

This list is not complete. Write down these clues and anything else you might have felt.

6. Anger triggers: Think over what happened. Can you see
   a cause for your anger? Here are some suggestions:

   I was treated unfairly or disrespectfully. Someone I
      care about was treated unfairly or disrespectfully.
      One or more of us were feeling harassed.
   My expectations were unmet.
   I felt powerless. I couldn't control the situation.
   My morals or values were offended.
   I felt stress and pressure. I was fatigued.
   My self-esteem was threatened.
   Someone else was thoughtless. Or incompetent. Or
      critical. Or irresponsible.
   Someone was interfering with my goals or plans.
   I was caught up in traffic or a long line at the
      market.
   I was very tired or fatigued.
   I behaved stupidly.
   Property was damaged or destroyed.

7. Again, this is not a complete list. Write down what you
   felt, thought, and did.

8. How long did you stay angry? A few minutes? Hours? All
   day?

9. Once the anger incident was over, how did you feel?

Tense, nervous

Guilty, remorseful

Depressed, sad

Mad at myself

Helpless

Embarrassed

Defeated

Ashamed of myself

Proud of myself

Relieved

10. Write a short summary about what you learned about your anger. What is it telling you that you need to do? What wisdom or insight is it sharing?

In the beginning, you'll very likely have to use your anger journal every day, just to become aware of your anger. Combined with your new awareness of anger clues and hot button anger triggers, the journal will help you to recognize the impulse that precedes your anger. That's the first step to healing what's causing your anger. By becoming conscious, you see that you have choices when your anger arises, including choosing to explore your anger. Here's how the anger journal worked for Joshua.

Joshua

Lately, 14-year-old Joshua has been getting more and more angry with his parents. At school, there's been lots of talk about going green, but Joshua hasn't been able to convince his parents to recycle. When he brings up the idea, his parents get defensive, and the three end up in an argument. Joshua's parents complain that storing the items before they're carted off would create a mess. Because there's no recycling pickup in their neighborhood, they also are unhappy about the time they would have to take to deliver the materials to the recycling center. These responses just sound like lame excuses to their son. As the result of his parents' resistance, Joshua has begun to put his parents down with snide, angry comments.

By observing himself over a week, and using his anger journal, Joshua recognizes his pattern of anger dumping—specifically, venting through his use of a harsh tone and language. In scanning his body for signals that his anger is on the way, he discovered that his primary clue is clenching his fists. Using his anger journal helped Joshua release the tension that was building in his body, and writing helped him to clarify his underlying feelings. In this particular situation, he realized that his anger over recycling was the result of an offense to his morals and values. Once he had his thoughts and feelings in order, Joshua stopped lashing out at his parents. Instead, he asked them to sit down and talk about his concerns. Feeling calm and confident about his views, Joshua could listen to his parents' concerns while expressing his own needs.

After this calm and quiet discussion, his parents understood how thoughtful he was about the future, and they appreciated his maturity in bringing the subject to them. Ultimately, Joshua and his parents compromised: They decided to give a household recycling program a trial period to gauge whether it would work for their family.

In this chapter, we have seen how mindfulness can help us to isolate the impulse that precedes the expression of our anger to give us more control over how we respond. But there is more to be gained from creating this quiet interval between the stimulus that provokes our anger and the behavior we choose to use in response. In Chapter 6, we'll learn to use that mindful space to uncover the unreasonable expectations and faulty thinking that may explain our anger—by understanding why we are getting angry, we may be able to eliminate some of the things that provoke us.

How Beliefs Play
a Role in Anger

You might think that when an everyday stressful event occurs, you simply react to it. For example, when someone cuts you off in traffic, you get angry. Actually, between the stressor and your reaction, there is a layer of thoughts and beliefs, which determine how you react. This theory is encapsulated in the A + B = C model proposed by American psychologist Albert Ellis (1913–2007). In the equation A + B = C,

- A = the activating event
- B = your beliefs
- C = the consequences

Basically, when a situation occurs (A), your beliefs and thoughts about the situation (B) produce your emotions and reactions (C).

Let's take a step back and consider the nature of feelings. Many people have the idea that feelings occur instinctively or involuntarily, out of human nature. This is true in the sense that a person might be capable of feeling love, anger, fear, and other emotions. However, the specific way we respond emotionally to an individual situation is a choice—usually an unconscious one. This choice arises naturally from our beliefs, which originated in earlier experiences.

So how do you know if your thoughts and beliefs are inciting your anger? To find out, tune in to what you say to yourself when your anger is triggered. The mindfulness skills we learned in Chapters 4 and 5 have helped us to create a space between the impulse that incites our anger and our response. When we look closely at that space, we may find some explanations for our anger. At your workplace, does the boss make unreasonable demands—or, if you're the boss, do your employees slack off after lunch? At home, are you often angry with your partner, your children, a particular child? Is one of your friends or neighbors always getting on your nerves?

In this chapter, I'm going to ask you to look more closely at the situations in which you become angry to see what information might be lying unrecognized behind these episodes. We don't need to go excavating to find these hidden messages and meanings within us. All we need to do is be mindful, and we'll see that they are revealing themselves to us all the time. By being present in our body, we can track our anger to the thoughts and beliefs that are no longer serving us and need to be changed for our own happiness and well-being.

MAKING ASSUMPTIONS ABOUT OTHER PEOPLE'S BEHAVIOR

People have a tendency to view a present event, especially an unpleasant one, through memories of the past. We may then react in a way that is out of proportion to the current situation or does not reflect it accurately. Consider the following hypothetical scenarios:

- In the morning, you and your wife agree on what to have for dinner. You pick up the necessary ingredients on your way home, but when you arrive, your wife says she wants to go out for dinner. You snarl, "You said you would cook.

Why did I go out of my way to get groceries, if you're not going to keep your part of the bargain? I can't depend on you to keep your promises."

- You and your husband both have hectic work schedules. You believe that if you don't do the household chores yourself, they won't get done. As you perform these tasks (e.g., doing laundry, paying bills, taking out the trash), you find yourself resentfully muttering, "Why am I always the person taking one for the team?"

- One night, right after work, you explain to your husband that your two children need to be transported to two different events on Saturday. You outline a plan for accomplishing this. When Saturday arrives, your husband has forgotten his role in the plan. "You never listen to me!" you accuse him.

- You've let your wife know that you would rather not spend time with the Joneses, a couple she knows from the neighborhood. You're getting ready for a relaxed weekend at home, when you hear her on the phone making a dinner date. Sure enough, it's with the Joneses. "I guess you like them better than you like me," you tell her.

When you find yourself responding to an event with anger, ask yourself, "What's the time line here? Am I seeing the situation as it is? Or am I bringing the past into the present?" Here are some clues that you are reacting to something in the past, beyond the present situation or offense:

- You can't let go of the angry energy in your body and move on, even after someone apologizes or explains.
- You're aware that you're having a habitual response.
- The language you use suggests that the issue is from the past—*never* and *always* turn up when you're complaining about single events.

- You view situations as black or white—all good or all bad, all or nothing.
- You tend to leap to the worst possible conclusions: catastrophic thinking.
- You blame the person rather than assessing the source of the problem more accurately—you overreact.

Ginny and Alice

On Monday, Ginny and Alice always have lunch together, and then they take a walk in the neighborhood to get some exercise and catch up on the last week. This Monday, Alice seems distracted while they're eating, and Ginny realizes at one point that Alice is hardly listening to her at all. She doesn't want to confront Alice, so she just carries on, even though she's mostly talking to herself.

As they leave the restaurant, Alice says, "I'm expecting an important phone call so I have to get back to the office right away. No walk today. See you soon." Her air kiss falls somewhere near Ginny's left ear, and she's off.

Ginny's disappointment quickly turns to anger. "Alice just doesn't care about me," she thinks. "If she doesn't want to be my friend anymore, she should just say so, instead of giving me the cold shoulder."

Does Ginny sound like you? Or would you think neutrally, "I wonder what's going on with Alice? I'll have to call her later and see if she's okay." It's important to take a step back from your emotions in situations like this one and move away from making assumptions and judgments.

Keep your mind open to the possibility that you are judging a situation based on experiences (especially habitual ones) from the past, even from your childhood. Consider the judgments in the scenarios at the beginning of this section:

- When your wife changes her mind about making dinner, you decide that you can't trust her word.
- When your husband doesn't help with the housework, you paint yourself as the only one making sacrifices in the relationship.
- When your husband forgets about transporting one of your children to an event, you conclude that he doesn't pay attention to what you say to him.
- When your wife invites the neighbors for dinner, you believe she's choosing them over you.

Can you see how your responses to these situations might seem extreme? There must be more going on here. Are *always* and *never* appropriate words to use here? Is coming home an hour late really a sign that your husband can't be trusted, or was there some particular time in the past when your husband—or someone else—let you down? Are you always making sacrifices for your relationship with your husband—or is it your boss who is making unreasonable demands on your time? Have you asked your husband to help? Does your husband never pay attention to what you say, or is this sense of not being heard something that trails back into your childhood?

The danger of interpreting the present through the past is that we don't have a chance to be in our current relationship and the present situation so that we can help it evolve. Habitual responses keep us stuck. Fresh responses to immediate circumstances, uncolored by the past, pave the way for closeness and growth. Mindfulness allows us to explore the feelings around our anger so that we can directly address issues from the past. Then they will no longer surface in our everyday lives.

Let's stay in the present for the moment, however. When you find yourself directing self-righteous anger toward another person, take a moment to explore the situation mindfully. Perhaps the circumstances are not what you think.

EXERCISE: ASSUMPTIONS MAY BE WRONG

1. On a sheet of paper draw a circle. We are going to create a pie chart representing possible explanations for the behavior you find objectionable.
2. Use lines to divide the circle into four sectors.
3. In each sector, or pie slice, indicate one conceivable explanation for the other party's behavior. For example, suppose that your husband arrived home an hour later than he said he would, so he is an hour late for the dinner you made. You are tempted to assume that your husband isn't worthy of your trust. But let's look at all the possibilities:

   He was stuck at the office on an important phone call with a client from another time zone.

   An accident on the highway caused heavy traffic or a detour.

   He stopped to run a few important errands for himself or for the household.

   His car suffered a flat tire or other mechanical emergency, requiring attention.

4. In that mindful space you've cleared between the angry impulse and your response, consider the other possible explanations for the behavior that is upsetting you—explanations that differ from the assumption you are inclined to make.

As you become more adept at assessing the facts behind your impulse to anger, you may no longer need the pie chart to consider alternative explanations. Mindfulness is a useful tool as you begin to examine the reality underlying your anger.

UNREALISTIC EXPECTATIONS

Another extremely common type of thinking that fuels anger is unrealistic expectations. In my private practice I have found that people get angry at least 8 to 10 times a day due to expectations—both small and large—that have gone unmet, whether it's because someone cut in front of them in line, they caught their boyfriend in a lie, the cable repairman showed up late, or they lost a parking spot to another driver who arrived a minute before them.

In relationships, unmet expectations take a variety of forms, many of which are unrealistic. For example, we might expect people to know what we need without our having to tell them. I call this the mind-reading expectation. The antidote for this expectation would be to tell yourself, "It's unrealistic to expect someone to read my mind. Therefore, I am responsible for communicating my needs here. I must recognize that nobody reads other people's minds."

Another example would be expecting others to keep every agreement they make. This expectation is not realistic. You cannot expect a 12-year-old, for instance, to make agreements and keep them all. Twelve-year-olds don't. They forget. They get caught up in a dozen other things. A person with this expectation could help herself by recognizing this reality and altering her expectations of others.

Another striking example of unrealistic expectations is perfectionism. Perfectionists think they have to be perfect; when they are not, they get angry. They also expect other people to be perfect—and get angry or impatient when others prove imperfect, as well.

Anita

At 43, Anita was a married professional with two young children. She had a demanding life, yet she stayed active and fit. One day, as Anita was rushing around her house, she tripped. Though she attempted to prevent herself from falling, she landed awkwardly on the floor, and her left leg broke. At first, slowing down to allow her leg to heal really drove her crazy. Anita was short tempered with her children and her husband. She felt confused by her mix of emotions.

When a therapist suggested that Anita try a mindfulness practice, she used the exercises from Chapter 3 to get in touch with all that was going on inside of her. She saw how thoroughly furious she was over this intrusion on her schedule. Anita also realized that she felt a loss of control over her life and a sense of helplessness and impotence. Anita had always prided herself on being the perfect mother and the perfect wife, in spite of the demands of her job, where she also had extremely high standards of performance. Acting out in response to these feelings would do nothing to resolve them—the anger would just keep recycling.

Instead, Anita needed to experience the painfulness of her feelings and the messages her body was sending through her emotions. As a result of this work, she became aware of some adjustments she needed to make to help herself cope while she healed. For example, she discovered that doing certain activities, like knitting and reading, gave her pleasure and reduced her stress during her convalescence.

Some people hold the expectation that they can do whatever they want—be late, for example—and people will just accept their behavior without a problem. This is also unrealistic. They think they should be forgiven for letting someone down or dumping anger on them just because they have done nice things in the past. This unrealistic expectation is called entitlement.

If we expect people to forgive us, but they get angry with us instead, we often get angry with them in return. Let's go back to our understanding of anger as a signal that something is wrong. The fact that our unmet expectations are causing us to experience anger shows us that what's wrong and needs changing is our thinking. Shifting our expectations about a person or a situation from unrealistic to realistic can greatly reduce the anger we feel and express.

THE IMPACT OF THE PAST

If you've become sick each time you've eaten ice cream, you won't be excited that the family is going out for sundaes. On the other hand, if you've bonded with your neighbor's new dog, you might be delighted when you're asked to care for the animal while your neighbor is on vacation. Past experiences often color our view of new situations, giving us associations that are either positive or negative.

The good news is that while past experiences can have a big influence on our current perceptions and responses, we are still in control. If we become aware of the past's influence, we can choose not to be a slave to our conditioning. We can get beyond our habitual thinking and view a situation with fresh eyes—a beginner's mind—which allows us to make new choices that can improve our lives.

Let's say you're driving home from an afternoon meeting just as the evening rush hour begins. Soon, a driver a little ahead of you darts into your lane. You have to slam on the brakes to keep a safe distance. You notice that you're feeling very agitated. Using all the tools of mindfulness, you pay attention to your inner feelings (sensations), such as faster breathing, a clenched jaw, and a knot in your stomach. You realize that in addition to being agitated, you are angry and a bit scared.

A memory surfaces. You receive mental images of a time when you drove into the back of a car after the driver stopped without notice. Separating the past from the present, you realize that the situation isn't as dangerous this time. You tell yourself that you can relax a bit. You see that you were getting so uptight because of the earlier incident.

Some questions that would be helpful to ask yourself in this type of situation are:

- Does this remind me of something?
- Can I remember a time when I felt like this before?

Overreacting in the present is a clue that there might be unresolved issues from the past. Especially at moments when you sense that you're overreacting, look at what is happening now and explore if it has a historic connection. If you feel that you need more assistance to get to past issues, consider working with a therapist, as my patient Rose did.

Rose

Because of a history of neglect by her parents during childhood, Rose tended to be anxious and overly protective of her son, Ryan. She would imagine the worst possible outcomes of everything he did. One set of painful memories involved Rose's junior high school ski trips. On these trips, Rose had felt clumsy because she lacked training and could not keep up with her friends. On one trip, Rose took a bad fall and broke her arm. So when Ryan asked if he could sign up for a weekend trip with his school's ski club, Rose flatly refused. She said that her son was likely to break his neck and die.

In a therapy session, I pointed out the exaggerated nature of Rose's fearful future fantasy. After many sessions, she eventually agreed to let Ryan go on the ski trip if her husband went as one of the escorts. Through our continued work together, this patient began to see the light about how she was projecting her own fears onto her son. Rose became determined to work through her abandonment issues and this old pattern.

One approach I used with Rose in therapy was to direct her to talk about her painful abandonment in childhood so she could experience the related feelings in her body while she was safe in the room with me, wanting to hear her truth. By acknowledging those feelings from the past and exploring her history in a safe environment, Rose began to heal. This exploration also eventually helped her to spot when events in her current life were triggering anger. At these points, Rose would become mindful about how she was behaving and reacting around Ryan. She worked on staying focused on what was actually occurring in the moment. At the same time, she allowed herself to feel her strong emotional response—but she did not let it trigger her old ways. As she made progress in therapy, Rose became motivated. She didn't want her son to grow up—as she had—lacking confidence about exploring the world.

Rose is a good example of how you can separate past from present, fully feel your feelings, see new choices, and even heal the original wound. By breaking the dysfunctional recycling of emotions, you can create a healthier life for yourself and others. I commend parents like Rose for all their hard work and their willingness to face personal issues. The children benefit, and the parents do too, as they grow through these issues and beyond. However, for all of the aware parents like Rose, there are many others who don't have a clue about how their behavior is limiting their children's sense of competence in daily life and fueling their family's anger.

REVISING BELIEFS THAT HAVE
OUTLIVED THEIR VALUE

Many of the beliefs that have the greatest impact on our lives are unconscious. They may have been quite useful in childhood, but we should have outgrown them, along with our clothes. These beliefs exist on a level outside of our awareness, yet they exert a tremendous amount of control over our behavior. Knowing that your beliefs drive your conduct to such an extreme degree, you can see why it is important to make it a point to take a close look at them.

The first step in examining your beliefs is to identify them. Tune in to what you say to yourself when you get angry. You might find that you hold beliefs such as the following:

- Relationships are risky because people always leave.
- I am valuable only when I am needed.
- I have to be perfect to be loved.
- It is weak to ask for help.
- My opinion doesn't matter.
- I always have to win.
- I must control my environment.
- I need to go along with others to keep the peace.
- Everyone is against me.

Once you have identified an unconscious belief, ask yourself the following questions about it:

- What is its origin?
- Does it still support me?
- Does it hold me back?
- Does it cause me to operate from a position of fear?
- Can I replace it with a more productive belief?

To heal, we must uncover and process unhealthy beliefs—releasing them and replacing them with new beliefs that support our well-being. To begin uncovering the unconscious thoughts and beliefs that may be triggering your anger, review the following list of faulty types of thinking, which have been compiled by widely respected family therapist Bryan Robinson in his book *Chained to the Desk*. Keep in mind that faulty thinking can lead you to view yourself in a distorted manner, act in ways that undermine your success, and act out in anger.

Types of Faulty Thinking

- Self-flawed thinking: Nothing I do is good enough. Something is wrong with me; I am inadequate, unworthy, and unlovable.
- Perfectionist thinking: Things have to be perfect for me to be happy, and nothing I ever do is good enough.
- All-or-nothing thinking: If I cannot be all things to all people, then I'm nothing. I can either spend time with my family or financially support them—not both. I'm either the best or the worst; there is no in between.
- Telescopic thinking: I always feel like a failure because I focus on and magnify my shortcomings and ignore my successes.
- Blurred-boundary thinking: It's hard for me to know when to stop, where to draw the line, and when to say no to others.
- People-pleasing thinking: If I can get others to like me, I'll feel better about myself.
- Pessimistic thinking: My life is chaotic and stressful and full of misery and despair; that's just the way life is.
- Catastrophic thinking: My life feels out of control and something terrible might happen, so I can't relax. I must be prepared by always expecting the worst.

- Helpless thinking: I am helpless to change my lifestyle. There is nothing I can do to change my schedule and slow down.
- Self-victimizing thinking: Other people and other situations are to blame for my overdoing, my stress, and my burnout.
- Resentful thinking: I am full of bitterness and resentment, and I will never forgive others for what they did to me. I am a victim of a demanding job, a needy family, or a society that says, "You can do it all."
- Resistance thinking: Life is an uphill battle, and I must fight to enforce my way, resist what I don't want, and cling to things to keep them as they are.
- Wishful thinking: I wish I could have the things I cannot have because the things I have are of no value. If only my situation would change, I could slow down and take better care of myself.
- Serious thinking: Playing and having fun are a waste of time because there's too much work that needs to be done.
- Externalized thinking: Happiness can be found in the external world. If the outer circumstances of my life would change, it would fix how I feel inside.

When your thinking doesn't promote your well-being, your mind can be your own worst enemy. Follow these steps to become mindful of the thoughts that are sabotaging your happiness, success, and well-being. Then you can begin to change your faulty thinking—and improve your life.

EXERCISE: PROMOTING THE THOUGHTS THAT PROMOTE WELL-BEING

1. Find a quiet place to sit, and focus your breathing.
2. Go through the list of types of faulty thinking, identify

which patterns you most often exhibit, and write them in your anger journal, leaving plenty of space around each item. Try to be brutally honest with yourself.

3. Reread your list. For each pattern of thinking, ask yourself, "How does this thought make me feel?" For example, if you possess self-flawed thinking, what body sensations and emotions do you experience when you think of yourself as unworthy, inadequate, and unlovable? Add these to your list.

4. Where did you acquire this thinking? Did someone say the message directly to you? Or did you get it from observing the way another person behaved or responded to your behavior?

5. To empower yourself, explore the opposite of each belief. In other words, replace the negative statement with its positive opposite. You might use a different color pen. For example, if you use telescopic thinking, focus on your successes instead of your shortcomings. If you think pessimistically, the opposite would be to tell yourself that you have the power to take charge of your life—that life can be what you decide to make it. As you focus on this new statement, notice how you feel. Does anything shift inside you?

6. Say the original statement again. Ask yourself, "Do I really want to continue thinking this way?" If not, scratch the original item off your list. "What can I do differently to begin changing this pattern? What might I do instead? Is there another type of thinking that I would prefer to adopt in its place?" Realize that you do, indeed, have the power to choose a different way.

7. To ground this new choice, create a chart with two columns, showing the old way on the left and the new way on the right, or a simple list of old and new thoughts (see the example below). Post it where you can see it

throughout your day. As you catch yourself relating to life in the old way, simply choose to shift to the new way and observe the change in how you feel.

Old thought: I'm not smart enough to apply for the new job. New thought: A lot of the requirements of the new job suit my work experience.

Ellen

Ellen, a single mother, came to see me when her stress was so extreme that her hair had started falling out. As we broke down the stressors in her life, it quickly became apparent that Ellen didn't know when to say no to the requests of others. Because of her willingness to help out, especially at her son's school, Ellen had gained a reputation as a person to go to when you needed something done. Between her demanding full-time job, raising her son, and the additional obligations she took on, Ellen was seriously overextended.

When we explored Ellen's blurred-boundary thinking, we discovered some of her motivations for always saying yes to people who asked for her assistance: She didn't want to jeopardize relationships, cause conflicts, or seem selfish or rude. Moreover, she wanted to appear as if she were keeping up with the moms who didn't work outside the home and who, therefore, had more time to devote to their children's school activities.

Fortunately, Ellen was now convinced that something had to change. I was able to guide her to a new thought: Having proper boundaries for her time and energy could be beneficial to her—and to others. She didn't need evidence beyond her hair loss that being less overworked and more relaxed would be better for her health. In addition, saying no to extra tasks would allow her to do higher-quality work on her existing commitments. Finally, by saying no, she would open up opportunities for others to take on new responsibilities—which could further their personal growth as well as help the project.

As I've touched on in this chapter, we acquire the vast majority of our personal beliefs in childhood, learning them from our parents, peers, and society—as well as our experiences and interactions with the key people in our early circle. In Chapter 7, we'll examine some of the profound wounds that these early experiences can inflict.

Anger and Childhood Wounds

Children are little mapmakers. As things happen to them and around them, they make meaning out of those events and place them on their internal map of the world, of how things are. The meaning they make often serves them in the short run—helping them cope with a confusing or painful experience—but it can do them a great disservice in the long run by making them overly fearful and protective.

Suppose Dad always looks at Jimmy's homework after dinner. Dad always finds something wrong, and when he does, he shouts insults at the boy—and frequently he gets out of his chair and swats Jimmy on the side of his head while calling him names that all mean stupid and lazy. Jimmy may see that his father is drinking from a can while he does this, but he's not likely to understand that Dad is an alcoholic who is now on his fourth beer since arriving home. Instead of concluding that his dad is unreasonable in this state, Jimmy is likely to believe that he deserves his father's rebukes and that all forms of criticism are meant to belittle him and may expose him to physical danger. For this reason, as an adult Jimmy may have an exaggerated fear of being criticized.

Childhood experiences can create thoughts and beliefs that live on into our adult years, filtering our perceptions and driving our behaviors until they are discovered, challenged, and—

if they are hurting us—released. Of course, some thoughts and beliefs cause our anger directly. Remember, anger is a healthy emotion that serves as a signal that something is wrong. Very often, what is wrong is how we are viewing a situation—our thoughts and beliefs about it. While some thoughts and beliefs may be related to a current event, most are the residue of past experiences and the meaning our mind and body gave to them. In this chapter, we'll explore some of the profound emotional impacts that childhood can have, but first, let's look more closely at what we learn about anger and other emotions as children.

ANGRY BEHAVIOR IS LEARNED AT HOME

The single greatest influence on the course of our lives is our family of origin. So many of our responses to life and personality characteristics, even as adults, started in our conditioning as children. Anger is no different. Let me be clear that this isn't about placing blame and rehashing the past, but it is about you understanding the reasons for the way you behave. Until you consciously choose to question and change your responses, you will continue operating on autopilot based on how you were raised. Before you can make changes, though, you must first acknowledge harmful behavior and accept it.

Few families know how to handle anger constructively. We don't address it as a society or place value on emotional education. But we humans don't come with an instruction manual. Although we tend to assume that we are born to be mothers and fathers, good parenting skills have to be learned and consciously applied to give our children the healthiest possible start in life.

Our childhood household determines our views of anger and how to handle it in two main ways. First, as children we observe how our parents and caregivers display anger. Whether you vent your anger on others or squelch it, pushing it down inside, you learned this from your parents and other role models. Did your father get mad and yell? Throw things? Threaten you with a belt? Did your mother silently withdraw and go blank? Or did she criticize and condemn, shame, and blame you? What do you do now when you feel rage?

We also learn about how to handle our anger through the explicit and implicit messages—ones that are implied though not spoken—that our parents send us when our own childhood anger shows up. Our parents often tell us directly—in no uncertain terms—that our feelings are not okay:

- "Stop your crying this instant!"
- "Don't take that attitude with me!"

We also hear messages through unpleasant experiences with our own or another's anger. Upsetting experiences come with implicit messages such as these:

- Anger is bad and should be avoided.
- There is no acceptable way to express your anger.
- If someone gets angry, someone else is going to get hurt.

It comes as no surprise, then, that we try to push away or deny our anger, given the many negative ideas about it that we carry around inside us. Parents teach children about anger not only through their own behavior but also by their responses to a child's expression of this emotion. Often the main message we learn about anger as children is that it is something to be feared.

Maybe, in your family, your mother was the only family member whose anger was accepted and tolerated. As a result, anytime you got angry you felt discomfort and anxiety; you made every effort to quash your anger. If you feared repercussions from your mother anytime you got mad, you would have to self-protect and bury your anger. Many children learn to say yes to unpleasant things so they can avoid being hurt in some way. This kind of behavior is actually a practical adaptation when you're small. Over time, the ideas you absorb about anger develop into a specific style of dealing with this feeling. If you can't express your anger now, then your parents probably discouraged you from doing so as a child. If you inappropriately vent or dump it on others, this is likely to be a style you observed in your childhood home.

Approval or disapproval from a parent becomes a gauge by which we judge the soundness of all of our feelings. If, as children, parents consistently soothed us when we felt anxious or afraid, we learned that it was okay to express those feelings. On the other hand, a parent who paid no attention to us or who disapproved of our emotional expression made us question if our feelings were valid.

And, of course, our parents taught us about anger and other feelings according to what they knew, based on their experiences and lessons taught to them by their own family. If you're a parent, you've likely been doing the same. And so goes the legacy of family anger.

What's so ironic about all of this is that when we're born, anger is a good thing. We innately know how to be angry in a way that serves us and brings us closer to others. We are hardwired to feel and express our needs—for babies, anger is absolutely a survival tool. Those early cries and screams say to our caregivers: "Feed me, clothe me, warm me, cradle me, attend to my needs." Because human infants are physically helpless, we must rely on our very first feelings of anger to communicate, "I need!" It is wonderful when attentive parents warmly and empathetically listen to our needful expressions. When our frustrated and furious outbursts elicit a loving response, this strengthens the attachment that is being formed in this crucial period.

In those early years, our outreach through anger functions to bring our caregivers toward us. In this way, anger is one of our earliest gifts, ensuring our survival by helping us signal for protection and love. Why, then, does our relationship with anger shift so dramatically later in life? And why do many of us find that anger in relationships so often fractures the bond instead of strengthening it? What can we do to bring anger back to its early status in our lives—a tool that helps us connect, not splinter apart?

As children, most of us found, over time, that anger became something that made everybody uneasy, especially parents and teachers, who tried to train us not to be angry. They repeatedly gave us the message that our anger and perhaps other emotions were not acceptable. Our relationship to anger began to change, as it no longer helped get our needs met or brought others toward us. In fact, anger sent them farther away. As we grew in size and maturity, our caregivers typically responded to our anger differently, worrying more about what they were experiencing than what we may have needed or wanted that caused the anger within us.

My mother is a good case in point. When I was a child, she often dismissed my anger, and that pattern continued during my youth. She worked six days a week, so I really looked forward to the plans we would make for her day off—to go shopping, to dine out, or sometimes to go to the zoo. But she would often cancel those plans, citing exhaustion. When I expressed disappointment and anger, my mother would quickly invalidate my feelings: "After everything I've done for you, how could you be so angry with me?" The message was clear: Your emotions are not okay with me and should be suppressed.

Some people leave the household of their childhood—as I did—with deep emotional wounds and the related anger. Like me, many people develop a false self to cope with their family situation.

THE FALSE SELF

As children, we want to please our parents. We want them to approve of us and accept us. We want their love. So we begin to curtail our feelings and repress them—pushing them down inside us until they are buried. We begin to live apart from our feelings, negating them anytime we think they may not get us the approval we crave. We create what many years ago famed psychoanalyst Dr. Donald Winnicott called the false self.

The false self is the person we think our parents and other important people in our lives will accept and love. Creating a false self is a clever coping skill, but it comes at a devastating cost. The more we cut off our true feelings, the less able we are to get in touch with them and the less we will know how we really feel about anything. We lose an important connection with who we are, and we start to become lost, although we may not recognize the fact. This false self is the person we present to the world. Over time it becomes like a role we play. It can look like the good girl, the good boy, the helper, the people pleaser, the martyr, the perfectionist, the entertainer, the funny one, and many more.

In her book *Necessary Losses*, author Judith Viorst says it best: "Parents unconsciously use and misuse their children. *Do well. Make me proud. Don't aggravate me.* The unspoken deal is this: *If you will bury the parts I don't like, then I will love you.* The unspoken choice is this: *Lose yourself or lose me*" (Viorst 1998 p 63, italics added).

My experience as a girl followed this pattern. After many painful interactions with my mother on her day off, I began to change my behavior. To get her attention, I developed my sense of humor. On the outside, I was constantly in a good mood, laughing with people, making jokes, even if I didn't think either the jokes or I were very funny. I was really good, and really fun, and you could never tell that I was seething underneath. That became my false self.

It was really scary to give that up, I'm telling you. In therapy, I came to see that I might be laughing, but I wasn't feeling funny or happy at all. To change the way I was behaving seemed dangerous, however. I thought: "What if I'm not funny? No one will like me or love me. If I'm not the life of the party—or making somebody else feel like they are because everything they say is so hilarious—I will be alone, rejected." I was terrified. On the other hand, I didn't like myself very much when I saw how dishonest I'd been—not only with others, but with myself, too. Little by little, I began to discover a more authentic self and share her with the world.

Like me, many children learn how to act as though they're not angry, but the anger hasn't actually gone away. We are not being honest, not speaking our truth. We are denying the reality that we or someone else is angry. Everyone is acting like they're not angry because that is what is socially acceptable. We act in a way that we believe will be approved of by others in our environment.

So, you might ask, what's wrong with this? It sounds harmonious enough. After all, we need to get along and live together in peace. If only it were that simple, we could all just stop there. But if you look around in your community, on the freeway, on the TV news—the violent state of our society, of our families, of our own hearts and minds—we can see that this strategy simply doesn't work. We have more personal struggles and anger today than ever before. That's because our feelings are an integral part of who we are.

We can become so conditioned to the false self that we believe that if we slip out from behind the mask and someone disapproves, it's all over for us. Any deviation from our role becomes a source of guilt or shame. Yet because this creation isn't true to who we really are, we become more and more angry the longer we confine ourselves to playing the part.

When we live our false self from an early age, the behavior

becomes entrenched. As adults, we are so afraid of our feelings that we behave like children, hiding our anger because we fear the disapproval of those around us. We become trapped, unable to mature and grow, re-creating our past. And ultimately the suppressed feelings don't stay hidden. Because they've never been resolved, they keep trying to push their way out.

A female acquaintance told me that she cried constantly when she was 6 years old. Her mother and father had divorced, and she no longer saw her father. Both her stepfather and mother had no patience with her tears, belittling her and insisting that she "stop all her crying." Years later, this woman lacks the resiliency to accept any kind of criticism or feedback. Not only that, she is constantly angry and judgmental of others' emotions and needs—but, sadly, she is the most critical of her own needs and vulnerabilities, seeing them as shameful flaws.

VICTIMHOOD THINKING

Besides developing a false self to present to the world, we may develop a false image of ourselves in response to childhood experiences. Victimhood thinking is one example, and it goes hand in hand with faulty thinking, which we discussed in Chapter 6. Here's how it works: Our thoughts and beliefs drive our self-talk, and our self-talk either empowers or disempowers us. Faulty thinking creates negative self-talk, which is disempowering. When you are disempowered, you feel like a victim—as if you have no control over the unhappy things in your life. Victimhood thinking leads you to take actions that don't give you what you desire. Empowering thoughts, on the other hand, put you in charge of your life, inspiring you to take positive actions.

Because being disempowered goes against what we really want in life, victimhood thinking causes a ton of anger. The source of anger for many people is the view that—in any given situation—they are the victim.

1. My boss makes unreasonable demands, but there are no jobs out there—I'm stuck with him, so I've got to do what he says, even if I'm breaking my back getting everything done, even if it turns out that he's making bad decisions. There's no way I can get another job.

2. My wife belittles everything I do. There's no point in talking to her about it because she thinks she's always right, and I don't want to get into a fight with her. She might leave, and I don't want to be alone. I'm stuck with her.

3. I don't have any friends—everyone thinks I'm homely and stupid, and they don't take the time to get to know me. It's just the way it's always been. That's my life.

In essence, we become victims any time we don't see that we have a choice. But we always have some power, in any circumstance, even if it's simply the power to choose how we think about it. This is one of the most important lessons we can learn to stop generating anger through our faulty thoughts—and it's one of the most important lessons we can teach our kids.

Having a victim mentality takes its toll on every area of your life. Think of it this way: Energy follows thought. Thinking like a victim (e.g., "Only bad things happen to me") creates negative energy in your body. But thinking like a person in charge of his or her life (e.g., "It's a great day; I'm looking forward to having lunch with my friend and working on that project") gives you upbeat energy. When you have upbeat energy, people are happy to be around you. When you're negative, on the other hand, people feel (and may tell you), "You drain my energy. You suck my life force." They will distance themselves from you because victims are a drag to be around.

Let's see how we could apply new thinking to the complaints we've just heard.

1. My boss makes unreasonable demands, but there are things I can learn from this situation. First, I can try to organize my time more efficiently so I'm not always breaking my back to get everything done. If I made a list of his demands, maybe we could negotiate some priorities. He needs to know that I'm doing my best to meet his expectations. Sure, the economy is bad, but I should keep an eye out. You never know when an opportunity might turn up that will get me out of here.

2. My wife belittles everything I do. I've let this go too long without talking to her about it. Perhaps we should seek out a moderator—a family therapist, or a minister, or an impartial friend—who could help us work out our problems. She must be unhappy, too—she's complaining all the time—and there must be a way for us to get along better.

3. I don't have any friends. I've spent a lot of energy thinking I'm homely and stupid, but maybe that's not true. No one can take the time to get to know me if I'm sitting on the couch by myself. I have to find an activity I enjoy and put myself in a place where I might meet other people like me.

The victim mentality is a great breeding ground for repressed anger. Let's look at another way that hidden childhood anger can reveal itself in adults.

PASSIVE-AGGRESSIVENESS

When children learn that their anger is unacceptable, they may also develop a passive-aggressive strategy for dealing with the world. Unable to express their anger—perhaps unaware it exists—they find ways to resist while appearing outwardly agreeable. Most of us have experienced this in at least one form: Someone asks for a favor that we would really rather not do, but we don't want to get in an argument or hurt the other person's feelings. We say yes, and then somehow or other, the favor never gets done.

With people who are truly passive-aggressive, however, this expands into a full-blown lifestyle that sabotages relationships because partners never know what they truly think and feel. A coping mechanism that helped them during childhood—when their power was truly limited—grows into a devastating liability in adulthood. Passive-aggressiveness deserves a more thorough examination, which I've provided in my book *8 Keys to Eliminating Passive-Aggressiveness.*

PASSIVITY

While passive-aggressive people appear to be passive, others are truly unable to express their emotions. Children who are abandoned or neglected may bury their anger and fear, making a promise to themselves never to be discarded again. Unfortunately, by doing this, children can unconsciously sentence themselves to a lifetime of neglect, making the choice to abandon themselves even when others are still very much available. This is how anger turns inward and leads to years or even a lifetime of passivity.

Christina

Christina was only 9 years old when her mother died. They had been very close, and Christina suffered deeply from the loss. In Christina's family, expressing grief was seen as a sign of weakness, and her father scolded her whenever he saw her crying. Like other people who are mourning a lost loved one, she also sometimes felt anger at the mother who abandoned her, and she acted out in school, where she was also scolded into silence. Christina's response was to turn away from emotions. She made a vow that she would never love someone as deeply as she had loved her mother.

Christina grew into a very attractive woman, and many men were drawn to her. She chose, however, not to open herself up to another person for fear of suffering the pain of another loss. Instead, she had a series of brief affairs. Sometimes she chose to partner with men who were married or otherwise unavailable for a serious relationship. If she mistakenly became involved with someone who cared for her more deeply, she found an excuse to end the relationship.

As an elderly woman, she was quite alone and came to therapy seeking some answer to her isolation from other people. She didn't realize that the source of the problem was 65 years in her past. She had never questioned whether the choice she made as a little girl continued to make sense for her in the long term. Instead, she had lived her entire life based on this early event.

When we don't feel our feelings, we hold ourselves back, often for years—if not, like Christina, for our entire lifetime. We can become consumed with passivity and, sadly, dramatically fail to live up to our potential. But let me be clear: Passivity is not ambivalence, laziness, or procrastination, although it may wear those masks. In a sentence, passivity is, "I know what I need to do but I don't do it."

Under the guise of passivity, some people are filled with a lifetime of anger that is focused inward because it is not allowed to escape outward. Passivity is a deep level of inaction rooted in feelings of self-doubt that sabotage the doing of what we say we want. Self-doubt is often a symptom of experiencing unmet needs in our past, making us question whether our needs were valid in the first place. Christina, for example, got no affection or comfort when she turned to her father for support after her mother's death, so she decided her feelings were wrong.

The passive habit of telling yourself "no" happens because it's the same message that's been drilled into you from a very early age. If as a child your cries for attention were met with dismissal or rejection by your parents, you'll understand that your needs are not important to the world and you'll stop expressing yourself, bury those hurt feelings in your body, store them in your brain, and cut yourself off from your emotions altogether. You become fixated on these bad feelings and experiences, and that allows you to avoid dealing with the problems and opportunities in your present life.

Some people suffering from passivity may have a depressed look about them, with slumped shoulders as if they're bearing the weight of the world. They may have slow speech and use a bland and limited vocabulary or speak in clichés like "cool," "fine," "whatever." Think of Eeyore from A. A. Milne's *Winnie-the-Pooh* with his trademark "Oh well" to every disappointment he endures. Other passive people can be control freaks, with taut, tense bodies. They are hyperbusy, speak quickly, and seemingly build themselves up by pushing others down.

Some passive people wait for the outside world to change to fit their needs, rather than acting on their internal desires to get what they want from the world. Instead of looking for a new job, they wait for their employer to promote them. Through passivity, they've lost all their power and relinquished emotional control of their life to others. Stranded without an internal emotional compass, they rely on others or outside factors for direction about where to go and how to get there.

With no sense of themselves and their own value, passive people may feel compelled to control how others perceive them, setting off a dangerous habit of pleasing others even when doing so sacrifices their own well-being or fixing the flaws or problems of friends and family to avoid experiencing their own. This self-inflicted powerlessness can give rise to deep depression, and it can also affect memory, stifle creativity, cause unhealthy sleep patterns, and set the foundation for alcoholism and other addictions.

AN ALTERNATIVE TO
BURYING OUR FEELINGS

At their core, all of these emotional approaches come down to the same thing: When we bury our feelings, we bury who we really are. We become a shallow representative of our real selves, one that no one can really connect to. We lose a dimension of our heart and our ability to give and receive love. And when we are being false, we can't be happy. That's what disconnecting from our feelings ultimately does. Believe me, when you discard a false self, you will absolutely feel the difference in your life, and so will those who want to connect to you. The same is true of victimhood thinking, passive-aggressiveness, and passivity. When you are able to access your emotions and express them openly and honestly, you'll have a lot more energy because acting in a dishonest way drains our zest for life, whether we're aware that it's happening or not.

As individuals and as families, we would be much better off just speaking the truth and dealing with the reality of our feelings. Avoiding anger doesn't prevent the pain; it just prolongs it.

The next chapter will take you, step by step, through processing your emotions within the context of an episode of anger. You will gain insight into what your anger reveals about your life—and learn tools for releasing and healing it.

CHAPTER 8

The Five Steps to Mindfully Releasing Your Anger

Long-suppressed anger may lie so deep you're not aware of it in your everyday life. Worried about periodic episodes of anger, you may explore your present circumstances and the feelings it evokes and still feel an underlying anger. These are fears and hurts and emotions that began in childhood. You can reach these emotions and release them so that you can move on to a more fruitful life, but it will take additional work. This chapter describes a strategy that has worked for many people.

As we've seen, our thoughts, feelings, and memories from past events and traumas that were not fully experienced remain unprocessed and lead to energy being blocked or trapped in the body. We then feel this blocked energy as tightness, tension, or pain. Typically, anger gets deposited in the upper back, shoulders, and neck; sadness in the upper chest and throat; and fear in the intestines and stomach. To free ourselves from the memories of these traumas and events, the associated emotions—stored deep within on an unconscious cellular level—need to be released.

STEP 1: GET YOUR ANGER PERCOLATING

The first step to moving old anger up and out is to awaken it—get it bubbling and stirring inside you, much the way coffee percolates inside an old-fashioned coffee maker. In the Starbucks era, we've lost track of the way our grandparents usually made coffee. They would fill a special pot or percolator with water and then insert a basket on a tube, which held the coffee grounds. As the water boiled, it bubbled up through the tube, filtering back into the pot through the coffee grounds. This would go on for several minutes until the coffee was brewed. In the same way, you can let your anger percolate through your consciousness until old memories and feelings emerge.

Breath work, one of the key tools of mindfulness, helps us accomplish this—it's the boiling water in our emotional percolation. Breath work awakens the cells and activates the body's own natural healing power to complete and integrate repressed experiences and release the energy in blocked or stagnant areas. If these feelings—the coffee grounds—stay stuck in our bodies, they can set the stage for a number of physical disorders. Slow, deep breathing also provides important health benefits. It both stimulates the immune system and relaxes the nervous system. Deep breaths help the lungs and blood vessels function better. Other benefits include lowering blood pressure, reducing anxiety and mild depression, and decreasing symptoms of asthma. Some forms of breath work can help relieve pain, increase energy, and reduce hot flashes.

Through focusing your attention on the breath, mindfulness also keeps you in the now—in your body—relaxing you and helping you tune in to the sensations, emotions, and other internal activities that tell you what is going on with you. Mindful breathing is one of the best ways to get in touch with your inner world and begin to hear its messages about your real experiences—showing you where you need to process out feelings and integrate new learning for a happier, healthier state of mind.

To get started, look over the two mindful breathing exercises below, customized for the two major anger styles.

For Anger Withholders

If you're a withholder, exploring your anger and other feelings can be a little like driving down a foggy road. You know there's pavement, but you're not quite sure which direction it's going to take. Mindfulness can be a powerful tool for withholders in getting through your emotional fogginess and finding clarity. This mindful breathing exercise will help you get in touch with and experience the anger and other feelings in your body. You'll learn what's really going on with you and what you want.

When you begin using this process, be aware that your feelings may not seem very intense. However, with time, you'll develop more skill and be more comfortable and confident. Even a feeling of emotional numbness can be explored. If you work with the sensation of feeling numb, emotions can eventually rise up from underneath the surface.

You'll want to choose a time when your anger was triggered or a situation was highly emotional, possibly because of underlying anger. To select a situation for the exercise below, you could consider Clues That You're Hiding Your Anger (see Chapter 5). Three very common indicators are fantasizing about a future disagreement, feeling tight or tense, and judging the other party critically. Other possible clues to anger include crying, headaches, a nervous stomach, shakiness, and breathing more rapidly.

Note: You might want to record a version of the following exercise, using your own voice or someone else's. Turn the recording off periodically during your session as you're examining your feelings and then back on whenever you need further prompting.

EXERCISE: A MINDFULNESS MEDITATION FOR ANGER WITHHOLDERS

1. Slow everything down. Take some deep breaths and think of a time when you became angry or had a strong emotional reaction that you suspect might be related to anger. You'll be working with these feelings during this mindfulness session.

2. Select a time and a space in which you won't be interrupted. Choose a comfortable chair, and sit quietly for a moment with your eyes closed. (Your eyes will remain closed throughout this exercise.) Continue to slow yourself down by taking several long, deep breaths, then begin to relax your body, starting with your face, moving to the shoulders and chest, your arms and hands, torso and buttocks, legs and feet. Relax everything.

3. Turn your attention to your breath. When you inhale, feel your nostrils widening, your chest expanding. First tighten and then relax your belly. Hold your breath to the count of three. One . . . two . . . three. Then exhale and really let all the air out. Continue in this manner, focusing on your breath. You're inhaling, holding your breath for three beats, and then exhaling. Just keep your attention on your breath.

4. If you find your mind straying from its attention on the breath, say the word "wandering." This will help you recognize that your mind is drifting, so you can focus once again on your breathing. This will keep you in your body, where you need to be.

5. Now think of the anger episode or the other strongly emotionally charged event that you chose. Make sure it is an experience—a time or personal interaction—when you were really mad. Bring to consciousness as many details as you can recall, such as who was there, what

they were wearing, what you were wearing, what was said, and so on. Picture it in your mind—and take your time. You may need to wait calmly and patiently for the feelings to surface.

6. Scan your body, still breathing deeply. Look for the strongest sensation or feeling that you have in your body. When you find something, name that part aloud. It might be your chest, or stomach, or shoulders—any part of your body. Explore the sensation in that area and see what emotional experience is within it. Is there a tingling in your body, a tension, tightness, or pressure? Do you feel heat or cold?

7. Now, sit quietly and follow the sensations to see if they lead to any feelings. Are you feeling frustrated, sad, mad, furious? Stay with any feelings as long as they last. Then move on to the next most intense feeling, and so on. Don't resist any feelings that come up. And don't judge them. Just allow them to arise, be felt, and then pass like clouds in the sky. See if your body needs to move; if so, let it move.

8. When there are no feelings left to explore, or you've been doing the breath work for at least 15 minutes, go back to focusing directly on the breath for 3 to 5 minutes. You want to take care to come out of this deeper consciousness slowly and gently. Take a few deep breaths, then wiggle your toes and fingers. When you're ready, open your eyes. Give yourself another quiet moment to regroup before going on with your day. If you wish, you could move directly to the anger journal exercises, described in Step 2.

Mindful breathing helps anger withholders get more in touch with the sensations and feelings associated with their anger. They are often largely out of touch with their angry feelings because of their tendency to deny or reject anger.

For Anger Dumpers

Mindful breathing serves a slightly different purpose for anger dumpers—it helps them to tolerate and regulate their anger rather than dumping the feelings immediately. If this is your anger style, acquiring this skill will be a huge step toward changing the way you deal with your upset.

Note that with the help of mindfulness, dumpers will typically find that their anger is masking other uncomfortable feelings that they've been avoiding—such as shame, sadness, grief, and powerlessness. Unconsciously, dumpers may have been defending against feeling these other difficult emotions by latching primarily onto the anger. These corresponding dark emotions can be related to events in the present or to incidents in the past that have left an internal hurt that still needs to be healed. If you have such wounds from the past, working through this chapter will help. However, you may still need additional therapy to adequately address these issues.

The following breath exercise can be helpful for gaining greater emotional clarity, developing more control over how you respond to your anger, and preventing you from lashing out at others. As you do the exercise, see if you notice particular areas of your body where you seem to be holding the feelings.

EXERCISE: A MINDFULNESS MEDITATION FOR ANGER DUMPERS

1. Scan your recent memories and pick an episode in which you became angry and reacted by dumping your livid feelings on someone else. What was the triggering event? What was your reaction?
2. Once you've chosen a situation, find a time and space in which you won't be interrupted for at least 15 minutes.

Choose a comfortable chair, close your eyes, and sit quietly for a moment as you begin to wind down with your
eyes closed.

3. Take some deep breaths and quiet yourself. Think of the
snow globe settling and inhale to the count of three:
one . . . two . . . three. Then exhale to the count of
three: one . . . two . . . three. Quietly bring yourself
into the now, letting go of any judgments. If your mind
wanders, simply say the word "wandering" and come
back to the present moment. This is not a time to try to
figure anything out. Take another breath, inhaling to
the count of three, then exhaling to three.

4. Feel the air going in and out of your nostrils. Notice your
chest and belly rising and falling rhythmically as you
breathe. As you focus on your breath, allow your body
to become more and more relaxed. Feel yourself slowing down. Keep slowing down more and more as you
breathe in a relaxed manner. There's no need to hurry
now. Just breathe in and out slowly for a minute or two,
bringing yourself fully into the present.

5. Now scan your body for feelings and sensations. Notice
all the activity that is taking place in your body. Then
recall the triggering incident as well as your reaction.
Keep breathing slowly. Think of yourself as a witness to
what you were experiencing. Being a witness in this case
means noticing and observing as well as reexperiencing
how you were feeling. As you recall these moments, try to
tap into the sensations or feelings that were in your body
during the original incident. See if you can recall the
signs of getting emotionally hijacked. What sensation or
feeling were you experiencing then? Attempt to access
the experience and keep breathing. If you cannot access
the earlier feelings, see if your body is tense or needs to
move. Review what comes up when you remember the

incident. Know that you do not need to be controlled by the experience; you can simply observe it without judgment.

6. Know that feelings naturally have a beginning, a middle, and an end. If your angry feelings are experienced in healthy ways, they will not go on forever. Realize that unless you learn to allow yourself to experience the feelings in a healthy way, there will be no freedom. You'll continue to be reactive instead of responsive, and your feelings will be in control. The child part of you will be in the driver's seat instead of your adult self. Dumpers tend to keep recycling the same old anger because it is not dealt with properly. (Anger dumping is not dealing with the problem effectively, even though you may kid yourself that it is.)

7. Even though the sensations and feelings are likely to be uncomfortable, just sit with them and breathe. Just allow yourself to experience your feelings and keep breathing slowly. You do not have to do anything about the feelings but breathe. Just stay in touch with the sensations and feelings for as long as you can manage. (Over time, keep working on staying with the sensations and feelings for longer and longer periods in the breath work meditation until you are able to fully experience them through to a conclusion. Then relax and just let the feelings dissipate.)

8. Now focus only on the angry eruption you had on that day. At this point, can you see other possible responses you could have chosen? Keep breathing and, for a few moments, think of an optimal way of responding to the situation. Picture yourself responding in this optimal way. See if any new feelings come with the optimal behavior. Sit with those feelings for another minute.

8. It's now time to clear your mind and just focus once again

on your breath. Notice it going in and out through your nostrils, in and out slowly. Sit quietly and just breathe in a relaxed manner for a minute or two as a conclusion to this exercise before gently bringing yourself to waking consciousness.

Through the breath exercise, were you able to stay with the angry feelings for a longer period of time? If so, that's great. If not, don't give up; just try the exercise again and again and you will gain more skill with time. By using this mindfulness routine consistently, you can gain greater and greater mastery over your response to anger and begin to connect to your inner world instead of dumping the angry feelings. In doing so, you will also likely identify other feelings that you hadn't been aware of earlier, further grounding you in your real experience and allowing you to free the blocked energy of anger in your body. The new energy will thrust you forward to pursue what you want in life, set boundaries, and stand up for yourself.

STEP 2: MOVE YOUR FEELINGS OUT THROUGH WRITING

The hands, feet, and voice are key channels for releasing emotional energy from the body. Therefore, writing—which connects the mind and the hands—can facilitate a powerful release. Especially if you use a pen or pencil and paper rather than a computer keyboard, writing can effectively get stuck emotions moving up and out of the body, thereby reducing or preventing the toxic emotional buildup that may be spilling out all over your life.

As a tool of mindfulness, writing slows you down and helps you get in touch with your inner world, enhancing self-discovery. Writing down your emotions—without judging them—is one of the quickest ways to become aware of what's going on inside you. Like the breathing exercises, writing will help you learn that feelings have a beginning, middle, and end. They do not last forever.

I call this exercise "no-judgment journaling" because writing what we truly think and feel, without being hindered by our own judgments or the fear of how others may view us, is the key to emotional freedom. When we're worried about what others will think, we can't be fully honest. Yet the release of the stagnant energy of stuck emotions can happen only by exploring our experience mindfully and expressing it accurately.

Therefore, in this exercise, you'll want to hold yourself to a standard of rigorous honesty. Equally important is to keep your journal private, out of the hands of others, sharing it with someone you trust only if you want to do that. Finally, don't worry about spelling, grammar, or punctuation. This writing is just for you, and correct language is not a necessary part of the exercise. Now that you've got the basic guidelines, let's get started.

EXERCISE: NO-JUDGMENT JOURNALING OF THOUGHTS AND FEELINGS

1. Find a quiet place where you will be physically comfortable as well as emotionally safe while you're writing, without scrutiny or interruption by others.

2. Begin by taking a few deep breaths. Continue to breathe slowly and deeply. When you're ready, focus your attention inside. As you breathe, silently state the intention to be a loving friend or steward to your life as you go through this process, allowing yourself the freedom to say anything you need to without your own judgment or criticism. The goal is to explore your experience completely, including your true thoughts and feelings about it.

3. Now bring to mind an angering incident, recalling the
details both during and after the event. Be as thorough
as you can, permitting whatever is inside you to pour out
in a stream of consciousness onto the page. Here are
some questions that may help:

- What happened? Who was involved?
- What part of the experience was most upsetting
  for you? For example, was there something you
  wanted or needed that you didn't get (an unmet
  need)? Or did something occur that you wish
  hadn't (a boundary that was crossed)?
- What were your thoughts and feelings about the
  situation? The other person? Yourself? This is the
  time to be 100 percent honest—no matter how
  spiteful, petty, immature, judgmental, unspiri-
  tual, or anything else it may sound. Don't hold
  anything back.
- Is there anything else you need to write about to
  get a complete picture of what happened?

This form of "emotional detox" works wonders in clearing out
the stored, toxic energy that leads to the recycling of self-limit-
ing thoughts and destructive behaviors. It's a safe, effective way
to experience and release powerful emotions like anger, sadness, grief, and jealousy, to name a few. Studies have confirmed
that men and women who vent their anger through writing
experience fewer signs of ill health.

EXERCISE: WRITE A LETTER—BUT DON'T MAIL IT

If journaling doesn't leave you feeling completely freed of negative emotions, you may need to express your feelings directly
to the person who provoked your pain or anger. The best way
to do this is in a letter that you don't actually send. Knowing

as you write the letter that you won't be sending it, you can be free to say what you really feel, without holding anything back. You'll want to practice rigorous honesty, leaving all judgments at the door.

The person you write to could be a parent, spouse, friend, former partner, and so on. As you write the letter, allow yourself to embody the anger you feel and steep in it. See what it's like to just be with the anger and not become reactive to it. If one letter isn't enough, you can keep writing letters to this person as long as the angry feelings continue. Remember, this letter is to help you; it isn't meant to be sent. Try not to edit your thoughts as you're writing. Sometimes using your nondominant hand can help you to bypass the left-brain censor we all have and access deeper feelings.

STEP 3: TELL YOUR STORY TO ANOTHER

A third way to mindfully explore and express your anger and other feelings that get generated in an upsetting incident is to tell your story to another person and truly be heard. Being validated by others in this way is a basic human need, so telling your story can help you make a powerful shift toward healing. Think back to a time when you went through pain, and there was no one to talk with about it. Didn't that make your burden feel heavier? Now contrast that with an experience of feeling fully listened to and heard. (Hopefully, you can identify such a positive, healing experience.) Being heard brings the realization that we are not alone, that others have felt as we do. We also realize that people care about our feelings. So, in addition to moving out feelings, talking helps connect us to the world and thus lessens our pain.

This is one of the main reasons why workshops and other small-group therapy settings can be so effective in helping people to have a breakthrough. For instance, in my weekend-long anger workshops, held several times a year, I see people releasing large amounts of anger and childhood shame. Because the atmosphere is one of respect and caring, everyone in the small group feels safe enough to share their most painful or shameful stories. Knowing that they may never see other participants again, inhibitions are typically low, and openness in sharing this kind of difficult content can be almost contagious. In these groups, you will frequently hear stories of physical or sexual abuse, alienation or abandonment by parents, and many other forms of serious childhood wounds.

Hearing that others have similar shameful experiences and realizing that you are not alone shifts self-judgment to self-acceptance. You understand that you're not so bad after all—you're just human. This can bring a major release of feelings and new understanding that leaves everyone feeling much more open and free to move forward in life without the burdens of the secrets and repressed feelings they've been carrying.

Talking with a therapist—alone or in a group—is the safest setting for telling your story, but a supportive friend may be able to help. Find a friend to assist you—someone who, as you share your most painful stories, will simply listen nonjudgmentally and not try to solve your problems or fix you in any way. It's important for them to understand that this is not an ordinary conversation. The goal is to get stuck emotions moving so you can begin releasing them.

EXERCISE: TELLING YOUR STORY

1. Explain the rules to the friend who is assisting you. Because telling your story without needing to explain or defend will produce the best results, you'll want to say what happened to you without being interrupted by the other person. The listener's job is merely to listen and

respond according to the instructions below. If there is no one in your life who meets this requirement, seek out a therapist, counselor, or clergy member to play this supportive role. Once your listener is present and familiar with the instructions, you're ready to begin.

2. Choose a painful experience to share, and tell your story to your listener, including the following:
     • The key details of what happened, including who was there, where it took place, the frame of mind you were in, and what each of you said. Recall it in as much detail as possible, using all of your senses.
     • All of the feelings you felt about it at the time and any others you feel now.
     • What boundaries of yours got breached or what needs went unmet.
     • What, if anything, you feel you did to contribute to the painful event or outcome.
     • How the choices you made that contributed to the problem seemed to be serving you at the time.

3. When you are finished sharing about your painful experience, your listener will gently say to you each of the following statements:
     • Thank you for sharing your experience with me.
     • I'm sorry that you suffered that pain.
     • I love and accept you anyway.

You can also do a version of this exercise on your own. Just find a quiet time and place, and begin with a few deep breaths to help you slow down and get into a contemplative state. When you're ready, visualize yourself sitting in a beautiful natural setting across from a wise and gentle listener. This can be anyone, alive or deceased, whom you feel comfortable telling your story to—a favorite grandparent, a long-lost friend, a spiritual being, or a historical figure you admire and feel safe with. Visualize the listener as being fully attentive and compassionate, and follow the script above.

This practice demonstrates one of the ways that psychotherapy can be an effective healing device. Many people never discuss their painful experiences and instead keep deep childhood shame hidden as an ugly secret for much or all of their lives. Shame can be a major source of anger because those who harbor shame tend to react defensively when anyone criticizes them or gives them the mildest feedback. They do this to divert attention away from those painful buried feelings. Therefore, the hallmarks of shame are hiding and secrecy, while anger is sometimes used to cover up shame.

When we have a caring person to share our shameful and otherwise painful stories with, one who is trained to listen nonjudgmentally without trying to fix us, we are able to fully express our experience and finally release those old, stored, toxic feelings. Free of those, we tend to shift our view of the original event and the beliefs we formed about ourselves as a result. The change is often profound. It can feel like a huge weight has been lifted.

STEP 4: FIND YOUR NEW TRUTH

To understand this a little better, we need to look again at what we do as children when traumas or attachment injuries occur. When children experience a trauma or an attachment wound, along with hurt feelings about it, they tell themselves a story about it to make sense of it and cope. This is both a help and a hindrance because the story is almost always limiting and based on fear. For example, a child who is left alone too long may feel abandoned. The belief that forms might be that people will always leave you, so don't get too attached.

Although this belief—what I'll call an old truth—may feel like a protection at the time, it will limit the experience of loving relationships later in life. Beliefs that are formed in response to an injury are always limiting and hinder us in getting what we really want in life.

If parents realize that their delay in response has caused an emotional injury in their child, they can go about quickly repairing the wound. They might apologize, reassure the child of their love, and set aside some time for loving attention. Noting how they had hurt the child, they might resolve to avoid such behavior or language again. Unfortunately, busy parents who are not sensitive or emotionally aware often ignore or just don't see our childhood woundings, and we, as children, form limiting beliefs in an attempt to avoid the pain. We go forward in our lives, burdened by these old truths, still needing that healing exchange with the person who wounded us. This is what psychologist Dr. Pat Ogden called, in a class she taught, a "missing experience." By helping us to reconnect with our thoughts and feelings, mindfulness is a way to get past the limiting beliefs and uncover the initial wound so that it can be cleansed and healed.

Step 4 is meant to set these wrongs right. The idea is to find a new truth for yourself, a message that will offset and replace the limiting belief—the old truth—that you developed as a child. This new truth is a message you needed to hear back then. Hearing that message now, even so many years later, can be an extremely liberating experience. The film *Good Will Hunting* provides a vivid example of the healing power of finding your new truth.

Will

Will (played by Matt Damon) is a brilliant and charismatic young man whose troubled childhood has left him with a criminal record and a solitary life at the working-class margins of Boston. When his genius for mathematics is discovered, he is assigned a psychologist, Sean Maguire (played by Robin Williams), to work through the issues that are blocking his success.

Besides Sean, Will's support team grows to include the mathematics professor, a new girlfriend, and, most surprisingly perhaps, one of the men in his circle of friends, who wants nothing more than to see Will move away. Yet Will can't seem to leave his past behind.

In the climax of the film, Sean confronts Will with Will's case file, replete with graphic photos of his young body after episodes of abuse. Sean shares stories from a similar past. Many children who experience physical or sexual abuse blame themselves. Not understanding why the abuse occurred, they conclude that they must somehow be responsible. They presume that they have done something to bring on the abuse, or blame themselves for not preventing or stopping it. Understanding this thinking, Sean concludes with the magic words, "It's not your fault." Will backs away again and again, but Sean insists, "It's not your fault. It's not your fault." Finally, the message gets through to Will, creating a shift in how he views his experience as well as himself. He falls sobbing into Sean's arms. These four simple words are enough to allow him to begin letting go of the old judgment that he was to blame.

He is no longer limited by his old belief. He gains valuable energy to explore his genius, and as we leave him, he's headed west to find his girlfriend.

It often takes a sensitive and aware therapist to help a patient transition from an old belief to a transforming new truth—it takes several steps to get there. If you've been reading this book with attention and the will to change, and you follow through, you have some of the tools to make your own way through this process: to take yourself back in time to the moment when the wounding took place and then to provide yourself with the message your parents failed to provide. This means identifying the childhood wound and giving yourself the missing experience that has the power to heal you and help you discover your new truth.

Accomplishing all this may be trickier without a therapist, but it can be done. I encourage you to relax into this exercise and not worry if it doesn't happen for you right away. You can always come back to it as you become more adept at the preliminary steps of identifying and feeling your sensations, emotions, and beliefs.

EXERCISE: PART I. FINDING YOUR HIDDEN WOUND

1. Go within. Choose a quiet time and place where you will not be disturbed by others for at least 15 minutes. Sit comfortably and take several deep breaths to slow down and begin.
2. Think of a time when you were extremely angry. Visualize the details using all of your senses. Experience them again now in your mind's eye.
3. As you recall the events, scan your body for sensations and explore them in detail. For example, if you have a tingling feeling, where are you tingling? In what part of your body? How intense is it?
4. Stay with the sensation. What other internal activities seem to go with it—are there emotions, images, memories? Perhaps there is a tightness or pain in your throat that you recognize as sadness, and you feel that you're going to cry. Maybe you feel like kicking and throwing a tantrum due to anger.
5. Focus on these new emotions, images, or memories. Are

any words associated with them? For example, you might find beliefs such as these:

    a. I have to be perfect to be loved.

    b. I'm never good enough.

    c. Everyone will always leave me, especially if I don't perform.

    d. Relationships are hurtful and should be avoided.

    e. You must have a career to be worthwhile.

6. Once you've gotten a clear sense about the meaning you made of the event or the belief that formed, write it down. Again, this might be a statement about yourself or about life, something someone else told you that you were or had to be.

7. Congratulate yourself for doing courageous and important work. Now that you've written down the meaning or belief that you made of your traumatic event, take a few deep breaths.

Unconscious beliefs are like an invisible, underlying script from which we unknowingly act out our lives. Because that belief has been limiting you, it's time to take your power back and rewrite the script so that the dialogue is more supportive and the plot's twists and turns are in your favor.

To find your new truth, I'm going to ask you to make an imaginative leap in which you engage in a dialogue with yourself. If you think of this using your rational, science-oriented brain, it might seem silly; you are, after all, one person—an integrated, whole being—not loose pieces. Yet we all have different strategies we use when confronted with different experiences, such as perceived threats. We identify these strategies or "parts" by the prominent characteristics of their response—for example, as the wounded child, the wiser self, the loving self, and so on.

The benefit of identifying these various parts and bringing them into dialogue is that we can mindfully explore our responses to life and see if they are fitting for the current situation or somehow rooted in the past. I'm going to ask you to use this idea as you engage in the following exercise—you may be surprised at the emotional power of the outcome.

EXERCISE: PART II. DISCOVERING YOUR NEW TRUTH

1. Picture yourself as a child, about the age you were when you first learned your limiting belief. Take a moment to see yourself in that time and place: How do you look? What are you wearing? What does your body language say? Then place the child in a quiet, safe, comfortable setting, maybe one from your childhood memory or imagination. Perhaps this is a garden, a bedroom, or a seashore. Once you have your setting, allow your senses to explore the surroundings.

2. Somewhere in this setting you find another person quietly sitting. You understand that this is a much older version of yourself, who is very wise. In your imagination, let the child join the wiser self, and allow the two to just sit together for a moment. Are their shoulders touching? Are they holding hands? How does it feel to be together?

3. Hear the wiser self talk to the child. The wiser self understands that the child experienced a trauma. Hear this wiser self explain that the child's interpretation of what happened was not correct, that what the child believed about the self or life was not true. The wiser self will say, "The truth is . . ." Now hear the words that complete this phrase. What do they say? Let

the words sound inside your head, then in your heart. When you're ready, jot the words down. They might be something like this:

- I can relax. I don't have to accomplish anything.
- I am special.
- I deserve to be happy.
- I deserve to have my needs met.

4. Now that you've got your new truth, thank both the child and the wiser parts of yourself for their willingness to participate. Both played their roles extremely well and helped to shed light in a profound way.

5. Sit quietly for a few minutes more, digesting and integrating what has transpired. When you're ready, move on with your day, or simply go to the next exercise.

This type of meditation is challenging to do without a professional therapist. The goal, however, remains important to achieve. If this doesn't work for you, simply try a different approach. One idea is to write a dialogue between the part of you that was hurt and the part of you that knows the truth about who you are—who can provide the healing experience. You'll recall that using your nondominant hand can provide access to deeper feelings. In this exercise, write the dialogue using your dominant hand as the hurt part and your nondominant hand as the wiser part.

You can also rewrite the script of what happened at the triggering event. Instead of things unfolding as they did, write a new, more positive ending. See someone—possibly the person who created the breach, but not necessarily so—come along and tell you that the belief you formed about the situation is not accurate. That the truth is . . . Allow yourself to go inside when filling in this blank.

With any form of this exercise, you will know when the words you've chosen are correct because you will feel a noticeable shift or release. Your feelings will lighten; your energy will increase. You won't view the world as negatively as you did before.

EXERCISE: PART III. EXPLORING YOUR NEW TRUTH

1. Settling yourself into a meditative state, sit with your newfound message. Has anything changed inside you after hearing from your wiser self? What sensations do you notice in your body? How about emotions? If there are new feelings, what do they seem to be saying? Do you notice any differences in your physical, mental, or emotional state?

2. Stay with this new way of being and take your time to explore how it feels, then think about how you might operate in the world with this new change. How would your body posture and movement look? How might you interact differently with others? How might you face your problems or life's challenges differently?

It's not realistic to do an exercise like this just once and expect to be totally free from a limiting belief that resulted from a wounding early in life. But we do become freer each time we process our pain and anger this way.

As time goes on, you may be ready to integrate this change further. Take a blank piece of paper and draw a line down the center. On the top left write "Old Truth," and on the top right write "New Truth." Make a list contrasting as many different aspects of your life as you can think of that have been affected by this new shift. Fill in each column, showing the differences between the old and the new. Be sure to consider many different areas of your life—such as work, relationships, self-esteem, parenting, personal growth, and goals. For example, if your missing experience is that you don't have to be perfect, that you are good enough exactly the way you are, then this might show up in your relationships in various ways. For instance, you might not need to be right all the time or have to know all the answers.

The key here is to keep being mindful and befriending your inner world, and eventually your inner world will come forward and make itself known to you.

Allow me to give you an example from my own life.

Andrea

As a young child, I learned from my mother that a career was the most important thing in a person's life. She literally told me, "You are nothing and no one without a career" and demonstrated her belief with her actions. She always put her work before everything else, including me and our family. I adopted this belief and carried it with me as I entered adulthood.

In the early years of my career, I was a driven workaholic. All of my self-esteem came from my work. I spent vast amounts of time attending seminars, creating workshops, and running my individual, couple, and group therapy practice. This took me away from my family and a balanced life—in truth, had I been living according to my own values instead of my mother's, a balanced life would have been more important to me.

It wasn't until the world economy went into a downturn several years later that I slowed down long enough to question the unconscious belief my mother had instilled in me. With big vacancies suddenly in my practice and the feelings of fear and mild depression that resulted, I had no choice but to begin facing the issue of where I derived my self-esteem. In working through this challenge, I was fortunate to uncover my missing experience: the understanding that I am of inherent value without having to do anything. My missing experience—my new truth—was "I am of value, with or without a career. I deserve to have a balanced life."

Since those self-discoveries, I take more time to be with family and friends. I also invest in exercise, vacations, and travel—with no guilt—because I know how important it is to recharge and rejuvenate.

STEP 5: PERFORM A RELEASE CEREMONY

A powerful way to continue the work you did in Step 4—to further let go of the wounding event, hurt and angry feelings, and limiting beliefs—is with an actual physical release. This will continue the process of moving old, toxic energy out of your body and psyche. Again, I urge you to engage in this symbolic effort even if it seems a bit childish to your grown-up mind. If you can suspend your distrust for just a few minutes, I believe you can feel the emotional impact of this exercise.

EXERCISE: PHYSICALLY RELEASING YOUR FEELINGS

1. If it's not too inconvenient, go to a beautiful place in nature where you can be alone with your thoughts for a while. An edge is ideal—the shore of an ocean, bank of a river, edge of a forest, or top of a hill or cliff.
2. Choose something natural in your surroundings that you can throw away—small rocks or medium-weight sticks usually serve best. Gather enough of the objects so that you'll have an ample supply when you need to send them flying.
3. When you're ready, take a few moments to go within.

Focus on your breathing and come into a quiet space in your heart.

4. Now think about the triggering event; see the images, feel the emotions, hear the old negative belief that has caused you so much anger or pain. Really get it all going in your body again.

5. Once the incident is being experienced in your body, take the first release object (rock or stick) and hold it to your heart. Imagine the energy of your experience draining from your body into the object.

6. Throw it as hard as you can away from you, out over the edge. Use your voice, too—scream, yell, roar, or make other noises—whatever allows you to get more of the energy out of your system.

7. Once you've done the release, if you still feel any charge in your body, throw another object, and continue throwing objects and vocalizing until all the energy is gone.

Remember, to get the most out of this exercise, you will need to work through the process in the previous steps before attempting to clear out energy with this type of ritual. By completing the steps through number 4 first, you are far more likely to get to the heart of the issue and thus to be ready to release it for good.

If this exercise doesn't appeal to you, you can experience the same kind of release in other ways. For example, find a private space to shake your limbs to release the negative energy. Or, standing up straight, use both hands to place a small, hard exercise ball against a wall. Lean into the ball between your hands and let the tension flow out from your arms and into the ball.

If you can't get to a place in nature like the ones described above, be creative. Do as much of the exercise as you can wherever you are and the rest using your imagination. It's been shown that the body and mind can't tell the difference between reality and imagination. In fact, many of the world's greatest athletes spend a part of their practice visualizing themselves performing perfectly rather than actually going through their regimen physically. So if your physical space is limited, for example, or you need to concern yourself with not disturbing others, you could simply go into a closed space where your voice will be confined, such as a closet or car. Then imagine yourself gathering the energy in an object and throwing it. As with the exercise above, repeat the visualization until you feel that all of the energy is gone.

There is no one way to do this exercise and reap its rewards. Think about what other ceremonies of release or letting go you could do. Again, be creative.

The release of anger you've experienced through your mindfulness work in this chapter marks an important turning point in your life. You're ready now to move in a more positive direction.

CHAPTER 9

Moving on to Forgiveness and Gratitude

The healing of childhood wounds and release of long-suppressed angers have a tremendously liberating effect. Suddenly, there's space in your emotional cupboard for new and more positive emotions, and your energy is also enhanced. By mindfully examining our feelings during this transition, we may be able to engage with two highly recommended emotions: forgiveness, which puts the final seal on the past episode, and gratitude, which puts a new spin on your outlook as you go forward to a richer and more rewarding life.

WHAT IS FORGIVENESS?

Forgiveness can be an essential part of healing, but healing can also happen without it. Although forgiveness sounds easy, people often find it a challenge—whether they are looking to forgive themselves or others. I think this is because forgiveness is misunderstood; most of us hold at least some misconceptions about it. Therefore, it's helpful to start our discussion by looking at what forgiveness is and isn't.

Forgiveness is the letting go of a grievance or judgment that we hold against someone else. When we release a grievance toward ourselves, it's called self-forgiveness.

Like anger, the issue of forgiveness comes up when we feel that we've been wronged. For example, you might resent all the hours your partner is spending at the office and his or her lack of free time to spend with you. You interpret your partner's behavior to mean that there's been a change of heart or feelings about you, and you feel slighted by the lack of attention. If you didn't feel offended by the behavior, there would be no need for forgiveness.

In Steps 4 and 5 of Chapter 8, you did exercises to fully experience and release harbored feelings. But even with those steps complete and your emotional charge over the event all but gone, it's possible that you haven't actually forgiven—or consciously let go of your grievance toward—the person whose actions played a part in causing your anger or pain. Without taking this additional step, the original wounding event can continue to tie up a portion of your life energy and keep you bound to the past. The result of forgiving, then, is greater acceptance and peace.

Misconceptions About Forgiveness

Misconception: Forgiveness means I am pardoning or excusing the actions of the other person—that I'm saying what he did was okay.

Truth: Forgiveness means accepting the reality of what happened and finding a way to live in a state of resolution with it and go on productively with your life.

Misconception: Forgiveness always means that I need to tell the other person that she is forgiven.

Truth: Whether you share your decision to forgive will be totally up to you. You can decide this on a case-by-case basis.

Misconception: Forgiveness means that I shouldn't have any more feelings about the situation.

Truth: Forgiveness can be a gradual process that starts with the intention to forgive. Its scope can grow as you release more and more feelings of anger or hurt. For example, you might forgive a spouse for being late for dinner; then, as you work through the underlying feelings, you might forgive the spouse's preoccupation with work.

Misconception: Forgiveness means that there is nothing further to work out in the relationship and that things between you are good now.

Truth: While you may decide to forgive the person, further discussion—as well as additional changes in your relationship—might be needed. Using the previous example, you might sit down to talk about your respective needs and find a way to spend more time together.

Misconception: Forgiveness means that I should forget that the incident ever happened.

Truth: With forgiveness, there is no need to forget because you can see the value in what you experienced. Having worked through the feelings and learned what you need to do to strengthen your boundaries or get your needs met, you are better able to take care of yourself in future situations. You will probably still remember but won't be bound by the incident in moving forward.

Misconception: Forgiveness means that I have to continue to include this person in my life.

Truth: There will be times when you will forgive someone but choose not to have the person in your life any longer.

Misconception: Forgiveness is something I do for someone else.

Truth: Forgiving another may very well ease the other
person's burden of guilt and help him or her to move on
from the incident, but it's not for that person's benefit
that you forgive. Forgiving someone else is done for yourself, to free yourself from the bonds created by holding
on to resentment, pain, and overabsorption with the past.
You do it to let that energy go so you can be in the present.

What Prevents People From Forgiving?

Forgiveness is a complicated decision, involving our feelings
about ourselves as well as our reactions to what someone else
did or said—or failed to do or say. You might be unwilling to
forgive a person because he or she never apologized for the
wrongdoing, but other reasons are more self-serving.

1. You're looking for retribution or revenge; in other
   words, it's not over.
2. You need to feel in control of your relationship, and you
   need to be right about every disagreement. You see yourself as the superior person—to forgive would mean losing face.
3. You don't know how to resolve the situation, so it's easier
   to hang on to the resentment, which can give you a sense
   of being strong and in control.
4. You want to stay connected to the person, and anger and
   resentment may not be positive but they still keep the
   link going.
5. It's a way to keep a distance.

6. You're addicted to adrenaline and the power and aliveness it provides.

7. You derive a sense of self from being a victim.

What's interesting about this list is that many of these needs and insecurities stem from a lack of connection with one's authentic experience—with one's real thoughts and feelings, which leads to understanding our boundaries and needs. When we examine our inner world and get to know more about ourselves, we're automatically more in control of our lives. The allure of revenge becomes far less compelling. Our need to be right decreases with a strengthened sense of self. We know how to connect to others in healthy ways instead of destructive ones. We don't seek to avoid our real feelings through an addiction to adrenaline or anything else. And we no longer like the idea of being a victim.

The Myth About Revenge

Speaking of revenge, studies have shown that this bent is actually hardwired in the brain—that certain pleasure centers get activated merely by the thought of punishing someone who we perceive has done us wrong (Cunningham 2004). Evolutionary psychologists believe this desire for revenge was a mechanism built into our early physiology to ensure our survival as a species. For a creature that benefits most by living in a group, taking retaliatory action against someone who has done harm and caused disruption to the group is an effective way of deterring future wrongdoings. Interestingly, however, although we usually fantasize that we'll feel better by exacting revenge, the study results show that we usually feel worse having done it. Revenge is no substitute for the true peace that comes from accepting what happened in the upsetting event, owning and experiencing our thoughts and feelings about it, then letting those feelings go as we move forward with a healthier sense of how to get our needs met.

Choosing to Forgive or Deciding Not To

Forgiveness can be completed only when we are able to see the whole picture of the situation that needs releasing. This refers to accepting what happened, understanding how and why it happened, and seeing all that came out of it—both the obvious bad and the not-so-obvious good. So, to forgive, we need to mindfully expand our view of what has happened.

Part of this expanded view includes a recognition and acceptance of our common humanity with all its flaws in perception and judgment. We all, at times, act from limiting beliefs and points of reference that have developed from our painful life experiences and no longer serve our best interests. These lead us to treat ourselves and others in ways that a more expanded or enlightened consciousness would not. Just about everyone has hurt someone else or made a mistake that harmed themselves—or both. This is part of life, part of how we learn and grow. From this standpoint, a powerful shift toward forgiveness can come from no other reason than that, if the tables were turned, we would like to be forgiven in such a situation.

Also, when we remain unforgiving of others, our mental impressions of them can be reduced to their offending actions, and we can be blinded to the good they bring or have added to our lives. Yet we all have good as well as less desirable aspects of ourselves that we bring to our relationships. In this case, holding on to our grievances can shortchange us from seeing the full truth and cause us to miss out on the good experiences with someone. Using mindfulness to consider our relationship may help us to revision our experience.

Note that sometimes we just do not feel willing to forgive. Perhaps the hurt went too deep, or the person was too abusive or expresses no regret for what happened. Give yourself time to consider if forgiveness feels right in this case, and see if you can get there later. You should not try to forgive prematurely, before you have identified, fully felt, expressed, and released the anger and pain caused by the person's actions—in other words, before working through Steps 1 through 4 in the process of releasing anger.

When you have no more feelings about the triggering event, and you feel that you are willing and ready to forgive, move on to the exercises below.

EXERCISE: HOW TO FORGIVE

1. Find a time and quiet place where you can be uninterrupted for at least 15 minutes.
2. Decide how you would like to express your forgiveness—in person or by writing a letter. As you work through this exercise, keep in mind that you will want to be selective as to which information you share with the other person, feeling free to keep any information to yourself.
3. Take a few deep breaths and then bring to mind the angering incident. Accept what happened. To be able to forgive, you need to acknowledge and accept the reality of what occurred. This means the events that took place as well as how you were affected. Denial will make any attempts at forgiveness mere lip service.
4. Acknowledge the growth you experienced as a result of what occurred. Having worked through Steps 1 to 5 of the anger-releasing process, you have experienced your thoughts and feelings and gained valuable insight into your underlying needs. In this step, take several moments to fully acknowledge how the triggering incident has led you to this growth. A benefit of this step is recognizing

that you are more than just that one painful incident. If it ever did, it will no longer define you. Not only did you survive it, but you have grown.

5. Now turn your thoughts to any others involved. Mindfulness can help you to understand how they experienced the situation. First, consider the limiting beliefs or skewed frame of reference that must have been in play for them to do what they did. What need were they trying to meet? Also, remind yourself that forgiving doesn't mean forgetting what you've learned or allowing yourself to be treated in the same way again. Further, wish them the same benefit of growth and learning that you have gained through this experience. You don't have to actually wish them well, only that they can learn and grow beyond the unmet needs and frame of reference that led them to their past actions.

6. Choose whether or not to express your forgiveness to the person. Often doing so can bring greater levels of peace to you both, but it is by no means a requirement for your healing, which is the number one reason to forgive.

7. Whether expressing your forgiveness of the person directly or only to yourself, say the words, "I forgive you" and add only as much explanation as you see benefits you and your relationship.

8. As a final step, congratulate yourself. Forgiving the other person is a wonderful way of honoring yourself. It affirms to the universe that you deserve to be happy. And there is no doubt that the peace and strength that come from forgiveness are key ingredients to a happy life.

When It's Yourself Whom You Need to Forgive

What about when you are the person you need to forgive? Forgiving ourselves can often be the hardest to do. While it's true that we are sometimes tough in our judgments of others, we're typically even more brutal on ourselves. We've all felt regret over actions we've done out of ignorance or ego that have harmed or upset others or hurt ourselves, sometimes catastrophically. If only there were a cosmic Undo button. Well, forgiveness and its subsequent step of making amends may be the next best thing.

When we acknowledge our mistakes, we tend to think harshly of ourselves. That's because we expect the best of ourselves—we want to be perfect in everything we do. To forgive ourselves requires letting go of this kind of perfectionism and adopting a different view and belief about ourselves—that life is for learning and that true perfection lies in always working to improve ourselves and not in avoiding mistakes. There's no such thing as being perfect, but we can still seek excellence. When we strive for perfection, all we'll see is flaws. This can be a hard pill to swallow because beating ourselves up feels so natural. Again, this likely goes back to our days in the tribe, when it was hardwired into our brain to not do anything that would disturb the well-being of the group.

When we make a mistake that causes harm to ourselves or others—and if we are sincere about wanting to make things better—we need to self-forgive. The reason is that punishing ourselves doesn't serve anyone. It only ties us to our past mistakes, keeping us wounded and small and unable to contribute positively to the people we've harmed (or anyone else). If we don't work mindfully through our feelings and move to self-forgiveness, we can be forever trapped in our anger, shame, guilt, sadness, and other negative thoughts and emotions. Self-forgiveness is a tool not just for anger but for all uncomfortable feelings.

I'd also like you to consider that even if you're no longer in the lives of those you've harmed and you can do nothing to improve their lives or make amends, the truth remains that you deserve to be happy. This requires self-forgiveness. The following exercise will walk you through the steps of forgiving your-self and then taking action to make amends.

EXERCISE: FORGIVING OURSELVES
AND MAKING AMENDS

Before we can release the guilt and other feelings that come when we have made a mistake, a few steps are required:

1. You need to own what you have done. This means both your actions and the consequences that resulted from them. When we fully accept our accountability for what happened, we are more readily able to take responsibility for our future choices.

2. Next, it's important to understand why you did what you did. Through emotional mindfulness, reexperience what you were feeling when the mistake was made. Do this compassionately yet responsibly, not looking for excuses or justifications but specifically for what need you were trying to meet, given the frame of reference you had at the time. When we understand our frame of reference, it becomes clear that we were doing the best we knew how to do. Learning what need we were trying to meet can lead us to find more constructive ways of meeting the same needs now and in the future.

3. Next, acknowledge all that you have learned in going through the triggering experience as well as all the personal work you have done on your thoughts and feelings. How are you better today than you were before the incident? What have you learned and how has that improved your life?

Once you have done these three steps, you may be ready to self-forgive. If so, continue with number 4. If you feel that atonement is required before you can forgive, jump to number 5 below.

4. State your self-forgiveness by simply saying, "I forgive myself," or a more descriptive affirmation that states your intention to forgive and move forward, rather than remaining stuck in self-flagellation. This could be something like, "I forgive myself for my errors, and allow myself to move forward today." Or perhaps, "The past is done; I cannot change it. Still, I can be a loving steward to my life today." Another wonderful affirmation you may want to try is the Serenity Prayer by Reinhold Niebuhr used in Alcoholics Anonymous. It helps us to focus on what is in our power to change as we move forward: "God grant me the serenity to accept the things I cannot change; courage to change the things I can; and wisdom to know the difference."

5. If others have been harmed by your choices or actions, you can communicate to those people your understanding of the damage you have done to them and apologize: "I'm sorry for the pain I caused you."

6. Next, you need to atone—to put your regret into action, to minimize the damage your actions have done—"to make your wrong a right." Atonement is very powerful; it can be a life-changing act.

   Use your creativity when choosing how you want to make amends. If you can't do something to directly affect those you harmed, help someone else who is in need. It's the best thing you can do. Find a way to make someone else's life better, not as a way to keep punishing yourself but as a way to let go of the punishment and move on with a productive life that adds value to the world. For example, if you have hurt someone's feelings by not listening to them in their hour of need, take the time to listen to someone who needs it. If you have caused someone physical harm, do something that helps someone to physically heal. Use your time, talents, skills, or money to benefit someone else who needs it.

7. Finally, we need to take what we have learned from our mistake and apply it toward our future actions. More than an intention to do better, you need to come up with a plan to keep yourself on track. Ask yourself, "What can I do to ensure I don't make the same mistake again?" This requires a dedicated commitment to staying mindful.

8. Now that you're doing all that you can to make things better, it may be easier to forgive yourself. Give it a try, knowing that no benefit or good can come from keeping yourself stuck in the disempowering pattern of self-punishment. Say, "I forgive myself for the mistakes I have made, and I allow myself to move forward in living my best."

9. Congratulate yourself for taking these steps to self-forgive. Realize that you deserve to be happy!

HAVE GRATITUDE

Negative thoughts and emotions lower our emotional energy. As we process our feelings, we have the opportunity to turn our minds to positive thoughts and emotions. Changing our emotional energy is done with our thoughts and, though it does take some willpower to want to feel better and take action, the remedy is really quite simple. It's gratitude. Gratitude can immediately help you shift your thoughts and energy out of the anger and victimhood trap and into a higher, more empowering frame of mind.

Having gratitude—focusing our thoughts on the things we are thankful for, on what we love—is so powerful, it feels just about divine to me. If your thoughts are of a positive nature, if they reflect gratitude, your energy will follow: There will be a spring in your step. You will feel uplifted and energized. It's the opposite of what victimhood thinking creates.

By uplifting us, gratitude gives us hope and inspires solutions. It brings us into a mode of collaboration rather than competition, which also makes finding solutions easier. It also helps us to perform better because when we're mindful of our gratitude, we're focusing on the joy in our lives big or small, our opportunities, and our abilities to create more abundance. In this state of mind, fear cannot exist and therefore won't impede our progress. With gratitude, we look for solutions, instead of the victim's self-defeating habit of wallowing in problems.

Regardless of your circumstances or the pain or loss you've been through, gratitude can make a positive difference in your life today. By finding even one small thing to be grateful for and holding that feeling for as few as 15 to 20 seconds, you can feel a dramatic uplift in your mood and physiology. Gratitude empowers you with joy.

Although gratitude is simple, that doesn't always mean it's easy. We often want to feel good before we take positive action, but in this case, we need to take one small action so that we can then feel good. Therefore, cultivating gratitude requires some will, discipline, and practice. It's where the rubber meets the road. You have to be willing to allow yourself to feel good, and you have to use your discipline to take the small step that will help you make the shift, even when you don't feel like it. It also takes practice to notice when you're offtrack and feeling fear, anger, or despair. It takes practice to shift your energy by choosing to put your attention on something that will make you feel better. I recommend the following exercise to cultivate gratitude—to establish it as an ingrained way of being.

EXERCISE: MAKE A DAILY GRATITUDE LIST

To build your gratitude muscle and make it a habit that you can rely on when things are tough, you'll need a formal routine to get started and keep it going.

1. Get yourself a small notebook that is just for gratitude. Label it your gratitude journal.

2. First thing in the morning, make a list of the things that you are thankful for. Think of everything that is good in your life—even if you don't have everything you want. Think of the big things, and the small ones. For example, maybe you've got excellent health, or are working on an interesting project, or are taking a new class you enjoy—maybe you're simply enjoying a delicious cup of coffee or tea as you read this before heading off to work. Even people who have very little can find something for which they are grateful.

3. If possible, carry your gratitude journal with you throughout the day, and add entries to it as you experience or remember things you are grateful for.

4. Before going to sleep at night, review the day's list.

Well, how was your day? Did you find that you actually began looking for the good in your life? How did appreciating what you have make you feel? How did those feelings change the way you behaved?

Although cultivating gratitude as a habit takes time, I am certain that if you try this exercise for even one day, you will be amazed at how much more uplifted you feel and how that feeling translates to more constructive behavior. Find a time and place that you can regularly work to develop this habit. For example, I find it easy to do gratitude work when I take a walk because I'm naturally so happy just to be outside. The magnitude of the impact of this thought process on our happiness and energy levels is truly amazing.

The power of gratitude can also work its magic on our relationships. Relationships suffer when we focus on the negative, while having gratitude for what others bring to our lives makes our relationships stronger as we express our appreciation. In this exercise, you'll have the opportunity to write letters to people it's easy for you to love as well as to those who have added benefit to your life in a less obvious way.

EXERCISE: WRITE A LETTER OF GRATITUDE

1. Take a quiet moment and think back over your life to the people you most love, admire, or otherwise appreciate— those who have made your life better in some way. They could include a parent, teacher, friend, or even a public figure or fictional character from your favorite book, TV show, or film. Make a list of as many people as you like and, when you're done, choose one of them to use for this exercise. Once you've got the person selected, write the name at the top of a new piece of paper.

2. Next, spend a few minutes reminiscing about this person and his or her meaning in your life. Think about the person's strengths, virtues, and other admirable qualities. How have they benefited you? Under the person's name, list the qualities you appreciate most—generous, insightful, kind—as well as the contributions the person has made to your life: Did he tell it to you straight when you needed to hear a difficult truth, or did she offer love and support during a time of need? Maybe this special person taught you to have boundaries and use your voice to tell others no. Think about what you are grateful for and how this person helped to positively shape who you are today.

3. Now write this person a letter, expressing your gratitude. There is no right way to do this—just open your heart and share your thoughts and feelings. Try to relax, have fun, and enjoy the loving energy that is flowing as you express your gratitude to this person. Then, if you like,

send the letter. If the person is deceased, fictional, or otherwise unreachable, post it on a blog, leave it on a grave, or burn it up in your own special ceremony.

4. Now repeat Steps 1 to 3 above with another person from your list. Or for an extra challenge, one in which you will positively stretch, think of a person who has helped shape your life by being antagonistic to you in some way. We sometimes call these people our "petty tyrants." Even if they bugged you to death, criticized, or humiliated you, see if you can find the benefit they added to your life. Write them a letter of gratitude for their contribution to who you have become and choose whether you want to send it.

5. Do this as often and with as many people as you like.

Jeannie

A patient, Jeannie, 42, wrote this gratitude letter to her mother:

Dear Mom,

I want to thank you for your example, even though it has taught me what not to do. Thank you for showing me that pleasing others and living according to their values is not what my life is supposed to be about. Doing things just to please others can be part of what I do—an important part that creates joy and connection as I give to those I love—yet it needs to be balanced with taking care of myself. Thank you for teaching me that I am of value, too. Looking back, I see how you always sacrificed yourself for everyone else—giving away everything you had and were to make life work for the rest of us. It's as though you felt that you somehow didn't count, that your life and fulfillment didn't matter. With all my heart, I wish that you had seen that it was important to make life good for yourself, too. From you I have learned one of the most important lessons of my life: that I have to make my life okay for me first, then I can give to others because I want to, not because I have to.

Released from the burden of your anger, you can now connect more easily with all of your emotions. Perhaps more important, you can connect with the important people in your life. Chapter 10 shows how the same mindfulness that has helped you to engage anger as a positive element of your experience can help your relationships to blossom with emotional freedom.

Mindfulness and the Emotional Freedom to Connect

"What would you have to give up and what would you gain if you stopped living your life to get back at your mother?" That was the question a psychologist put to me at a workshop I was attending, and it changed my life.

I had spent my first 17 years trying to win my mother's love, at the same time that she shamed and blamed me in an effort to keep me from enjoying other relationships. I spent the next 17 years getting back at her. It took me a long time to complete my bachelor's degree because I deliberately flunked out of courses so that she would be humiliated. And, of course, I briefly married so that she would have to pay for an extravagant wedding. The quick divorce added to her pain.

Now for the first time, someone had called me out on my behavior. It was a lightbulb experience. All at once, I saw that my passive expressions of anger were focusing my energy on hurting those close to me. No room was left for love, compassion, and understanding. I may have hurt my parents and others, but I was also hurting myself. Worse still, I was shutting myself off from relationships that could make me happy.

Therapy helped me to slow down and mindfully explore my feelings and to overcome my fear of expressing them. I learned how to break through my limiting beliefs—for example, that I needed to be funny and to achieve great things in order to be loved—and to create loving relationships and an authentic life. By exploring and releasing anger—much of it decades old—I was also able to open myself to an intimacy with others that I had never experienced.

Of course, while the transformation can be described in just a page or so of type, it actually takes a lot of time and effort. Perhaps the most difficult thing of all is that you must look at yourself honestly, access your feelings, and learn to process and release them. It's not as simple as venting your feelings of rage or batting around a symbolic punching bag or taking a walk to let off steam. You need to understand how anger operates and to apply those insights in ways that use your anger productively to increase your self-knowledge and improve your communication with family, friends, and other important people in your life. Even more time must be spent in mindful exploration of deeply embedded childhood wounds and the pockets of suppressed anger around them, so that you can be freed of old, limiting ideas about yourself and your relationships.

Consider the alternative, however: the hours—the years—lost to recycling old angers and dealing with the resulting anxieties, illnesses, and relationship problems. Let me assure you that your investment in exploring your anger, learning to express it productively, and then releasing it is a pretty sweet deal, costwise—and it will pay dividends many years into the future, not just for you but for everyone you interact with.

When you understand your anger, you can discover what you need to improve your well-being and direct your responses to help you achieve your goals. By releasing old angers, you tap into a reservoir of energy that brings renewed vigor and excitement to your life. In your new emotional freedom, you can reach out to people—those who are already part of your life and others you will meet—with a new openness and vulnerability that allows intimacy to develop.

With the knowledge and experience you've gained through

examining your own anger and learning how to release it effectively, you have some of the essential tools you need to take a more proactive approach to life. Let's review some of the strategies we've learned in dealing with our anger:

- Although society encourages us to suppress our anger, doing that creates a stash of explosive feelings that will affect our lives in any number of ways, from physical illness and depression to all sorts of self-defeating behaviors.
- Anger brings us important messages that, when acted upon, can help us live happier, healthier, and more fulfilled lives.
- If we learn to identify the space between the sensations or feelings of anger and our response, we can avoid mindless reactivity.
- By controlling the impulsive response, we can consider the situation and choose to speak or act in ways that serve us best.
- Often our anger is triggered by assumptions and expectations based on our notions about the past, rather than dealing directly with actual reality.
- Using the tools of mindfulness to release our anger is the way to move forward in a spirit of forgiveness and gratitude.

These very same tools can help us to change the way we interact with the significant people in our lives so that we can build the loving relationships that are at the heart of the life we envision for ourselves. That's because how we handle anger and conflict plays a key role in the success of our relationships—rewarding connections are incompatible with suppressed emotions and restricted communication.

Mindfulness is the key. Let's begin by examining the reactive strategies that dominate so many relationships, so that we understand the behavior we are determined to change.

HOW REACTIVE BEHAVIOR
DAMAGES RELATIONSHIPS

We have seen how the fight-or-flight response—built into our genetic code from the beginning of human life—can diminish our chances of dealing effectively with our anger. Stress hormones flood our body, shutting down the rational part of our brain, the neocortex. We run and hide or attack and deny. What we don't do is mindfully examine what's happening and consciously choose how to respond.

The same thing can happen in relationships: A good friend says something hurtful; a romantic partner seems remote and uninvolved; a child is ornery and upset; a boss or coworker makes a new demand on top of an already packed agenda. The first sensation in any of these scenarios may be an acceleration of your heartbeat, a flush of heat through your body and face. When you're in a reactive state, these sensations can propel you to respond in a destructive sequence.

Instead of looking at what a friend said to see whether the apparent insult was intended, you might return the perceived volley with an insult of your own. Instead of asking your partner what's been going on to make him or her seem withdrawn, you may make accusations or pull away. Instead of helping the child to calm down so that you can determine the cause of distress, you most likely will punish or threaten. Instead of explaining the challenges of your workload, you resentfully accept the addition.

When in a reactive mode, you can turn trivial things into full-blown crises. Suppose your friend says, "This book is probably too serious for you," and you assume she meant that your mental powers were not up to the challenge. Maybe she was just thinking that the books you usually talk about are lighter fare. What does she mean by *serious*? Maybe the book is an academic tome you wouldn't enjoy. "I didn't realize you thought I was stupid," is not a productive response. You might say, "Tell me more about it and let me decide." But you're not likely to do that if you're the captive of reactivity.

In that mode, you're also likely to have a one-sided conversation, even if two people are talking.

Jake: You haven't said a word since you got home. What did I do wrong now?

Amy: I had a bad day at work.

Jake: Just tell me. I know the garage is a little messy. I'll get to it this weekend.

Amy: I didn't even notice. I'm too tired.

Jake: You know, it seems like you're always tired these days. At least at home. What are you doing at work that makes you so tired?

Amy: Jake, I had a bad day. Let go of it, will you?

When people try to hold a discussion while one or both are in a reactive mode, nothing is gained. Sometimes, people will talk over each other, so they literally can't hear what the other person is saying, but even if only one person speaks at a time, the other may not be listening. Too often, the silent partner is thinking about what he or she can say next to win the discussion. When that happens, everybody loses because no one is really heard.

Obviously, in reactive mode, people pay no real attention to the other person, but they're also not aware of their own words, tone of voice, or body language. Once you're caught up in the reactive mode, you may be powerless to stop it. It's like going down a slide. Once you've climbed to the top of the ladder and pushed off into the chute, there's no way to stop until you reach the bottom. Often, even if your partner isn't reactive to start, he or she may move in that direction if reactivity is your habitual mode—you can hear a bit of that in Amy's final com-

ment, "Let go of it." Or partners may shut themselves off completely, feeling safe in their silence.

Reactivity leads to a relationship in which one or both
partners walk on eggshells for fear of setting off a new angry
exchange. Although there may be no physical violence, it's an
abusive environment nevertheless. Worse still, the real problems—the disagreements and conflicts underlying the heated
exchanges—are never revealed. As you've learned throughout
this book, suppressing emotions is not healthy or productive.
The same is true in relationships. True personal connection
and intimacy require open and honest communication.

In our hyperactive society, with stimuli bombarding us from
every corner, it's easy to fall back on reactivity. The new key-
word of contemporary culture is *multitasking*. We're just not
plugged in unless we're doing several things at once—watching TV while we check the weather on our tablet, and catching
up with text messages on our smartphone, all while we're fixing
dinner and our kid is asking questions about his homework.
This leaves little time for self-reflection, much less the thoughtful process of building our connections to other people.

USING MINDFULNESS IN YOUR RELATIONSHIPS

Mindfulness is the opposite of reactive behavior. It is a skill that
you can practice, and as you master it, you will become rooted
in the present, paying attention to your words, your feelings,
your behaviors—and especially how they are all affecting the
people around you. Instead of surrendering to pure reflex, you
will be able to slow down and take conscious control of your
responses. The impulse-control strategies discussed in Chapter
5 will be enormously useful here. By taking the time to notice
the knot forming in your stomach or the heat flushing your
face and to open the messages these sensations carry, you can

respond thoughtfully and productively instead of arguing or evading or pretending that everything is all right if it isn't.

Mindfulness is your most effective tool as you take on the challenge of remaking the way you interact with others in your life so that you can open the door to a new intimacy with people in every area—from friends, acquaintances, and coworkers to parents, siblings, children, and romantic partners.

Why is mindfulness so necessary? Because good relationships don't happen by accident. True, some of us may be better equipped with good relationship skills from our childhood conditioning and role models, but for the vast majority of us, achieving happy, healthy relationships involves a big learning curve and a lot of hard work. Getting there requires first becoming clear about where "there" is, by asking ourselves what a healthy, happy relationship looks like. Does it mean the absence of conflict and always seeing eye to eye? Or is it a relationship in which our needs and objectives will sometimes conflict, but we'll know how to interact with each other to resolve our differences in a respectful and empathetic way?

Of course, it's the latter—as individuals, because no two of us are exactly alike, there is no possibility that we will perceive life the same way all the time or even much of the time. And though this fact is obvious, somehow we always seem to hope for and expect that relationships will be easy and conflict free. Those who pursue that dream are doomed to disappointment.

We can, however, learn to approach others in a way that focuses on understanding where they are coming from and caring about their well-being in every situation. In fact, it's our responsibility to do so. It's okay to pursue our own goals and pleasures, but if we truly care about someone else—friend, relative, or lover—we should be putting the same energy into helping them get what they need or want. With this attitude and the skills that help to put it into action, you will be amazed at how rapidly anger is replaced by communication and closeness.

THE RESPONSIBILITY OF MINDFULNESS

Oprah Winfrey has said that she posts signs in her home, office, and makeup room that say, "Please take responsibility for the energy you bring into this space." I would love to see this sign in all the places where people interact. Our emotions—including anger—create an energy that we bring with us everywhere we go. This energy can have a powerful effect on those with whom we interact.

Mindfulness is a sound way to implement this sage piece of advice, giving us the presence of mind to take responsibility for the energy we bring to our relationships. We need to be aware of what we're doing and saying, to pay attention to how we're responding to the world around us—and how it's responding to us—and to take responsibility for our thoughts, words, and actions. This is the only way we can achieve true power over ourselves and create our lives more intentionally. Mindfulness helps to foster patience, compassion, and wisdom, good qualities to promote our own happiness and help us become a positive force in the lives of others.

When we interact with others in a reactive mode, we are basically giving up control to the other person's words or actions, to our own inflamed feelings or our limiting and irrational beliefs, and to the chemicals released in our bodies as the result of an ancient fight-or-flight defense mechanism. We make assumptions that may or may not be true, and we throw up verbal walls of defensiveness, even when we're not under attack. We're acting as if we have no power over the situation or our behavior. Whatever the outcome, someone else is to blame for pushing our buttons and making us feel and act the way we do.

The truth is just the opposite. We may not be able to control everything in our environment. We certainly cannot control how other people feel or what they think—although some people will try. We do, however, have power over how we view the situation, what information we seek about it, and how we choose to respond with our behaviors and words. You do choose, even if your choice is to blame others for your success or failure in life and relationships. You can begin to improve your situation only when you accept responsibility for it.

This includes being accountable for the harmful or destructive behaviors that may have been part of your past. It doesn't, however, mean that you are harmful or destructive. Once you are mindful of what you have done—and of how you are presently affecting the world around you—you can change. Just as you learned to step in between your anger trigger and your response, you can learn how to pause before you engage in the negative behaviors that are harming you as much as the people around you.

In our anger work, we saw that childhood experiences—even those we don't clearly remember—can make us feel that we do not deserve the happiness we seek. If you haven't already discarded this notion, it's high time you did. As I've said before, you deserve to be happy. In fact, everyone does. We all are worthy of the comfort, pleasure, and support that we can gain when we form relationships that are honest and emotionally sound. And the only thing standing in the way of achieving this goal is you. Of course, you will need to change the destructive patterns that are not cultivating the relationships you want, and that's always a challenge, particularly when you're trying to change behavior that was molded in childhood. You can move forward, though, if you keep in mind the rewards that await you if you can repair the damage you've done to existing relationships or create new ones on a healthier footing.

To accept responsibility for what you do, you need to start with a mindful review of the role that anger has played in your relationships. If you examine yourself and your interactions rigorously, you will be able to identify the problems. This is a sort of relationship to do list. The biggest challenge is to make and keep an enduring commitment to change the way you think and behave. In exchange, you will take back the power over your life. What you have accomplished over the course of this book in understanding your anger and releasing it productively can be invested now in transforming your relationships with others.

To get started taking responsibility for the choices you've made in your relationships, do the following exercise.

EXERCISE: MAKE A HARMFUL BEHAVIOR INVENTORY

Alcoholics Anonymous has its members make an inventory of people they have hurt. You can also make an inventory of people who have incited your anger and who, as a result, you have hurt. This will be especially helpful in gaining awareness of your current patterns in your relationships, particularly if the anger revealed in the exchange hasn't yet been processed and released. So make a list and, for each person on the list, answer these questions:

- What did the person do to anger you?
- How did you respond? (How did you feel at the time? What did you say? Do?)
- Looking back, what can you see was your responsibility in how things went?
- If you could speak to the person now, what would you say? What might you do differently?

As you write about different people, see if any patterns are emerging related to what has provoked your anger over the years as well as patterns in your response. Keep a record of these patterns as you continue working through the list. Are many of your angering incidents related to criticism, rudeness, or irresponsibility in others? Unfairness or injustice? Denial, entitlement, or incompetence? Now look at the patterns in your response. Did you become defensive and return the attack? Withdraw from the argument and put up a wall? This exercise can be very beneficial in giving you a new awareness of where you need to do some work, to investigate and release old hurts and issues that you haven't yet addressed, and to see how you contribute to the dis-ease in your most important relationships. This is the first step in consciously—mindfully—interacting in ways that best support you and those you love. It all begins with intent.

MAKING A MINDFUL CONNECTION

The classic phrase buried in so many apologies is "didn't mean to": "I didn't mean to hurt your feelings," "I didn't mean to make you angry," "I didn't mean to upset you." The unspoken—and perhaps unacknowledged—message is, "I wasn't paying any attention to you when I said or did whatever created a problem for you."

While there are certainly cases in which we're honestly unaware of a button we may be pushing or a wound we may be reopening, too often, these unintentional slights result not from having the wrong intention but from having no intention at all. Being unaware of the emotions of important others in our life has the same negative consequences as being unaware of our own feelings. You can't gain true emotional freedom without identifying and attending to your emotions, and you can't grow a true relationship without attending to the feelings of those you say you care about.

Think about the couple we met in Chapter 1 and again in Chapter 5: Stacey was looking forward to a chance to meet her neighbors at a Saturday brunch, and Keith just wanted to stay home and watch a movie. Lacking a mindful approach to anger, neither had achieved the emotional freedom to express needs openly, and both of them ended up angry and hurt. Neither was paying attention to the other person's needs in this situation.

But, what if instead of getting angry at Keith and pressuring him to go, Stacey said, "I respect that you work hard all week and need some free time on weekends. The thing is, I was hoping the mixer would help me make friends so I won't be so lonely when you're not around." Or if Keith—instead of silently and resentfully agreeing—had said, "I was looking forward to watching a movie and cuddling on the couch for a couple of hours, with the boys gone. I miss those times before we were parents."

Imagine what might have happened if Keith and Stacey had talked out their differences. Maybe they would have compromised—spending an hour at the mixer and then coming home to watch TV. Maybe they would have agreed that it was okay for Stacey to go on her own—it might even have made it easier to connect with new people. Any outcome would have been better than the actual result. He went along, but resentfully, and she felt he had no concern about her isolation.

Neither Stacey nor Keith had developed an attitude of mindfulness in their relationship. Their intentions were focused on their own needs, rather than considering the goals of the other. Certainly, neither of them intended to hurt the other person, but neither did they intend to extend to the other any love or concern.

Having a mindful relationship means being thoughtful about each of your relationships: What do you want from this connection? How do you truly feel about this person? Once you decide that you want this person for a partner—or perhaps a friend—keep that intention in mind when you communicate with him or her.

In romantic partnerships, keeping your love in mind is particularly important at those moments when you disagree or when you find yourselves in conflict. Your long-term intentions about this person should be uppermost. But they can also be a feature of your everyday routine: Bring a positive energy to your encounters, and you will quickly see the benefits.

A WIN-WIN GOAL FOR CONFLICTS

Being mindful of the other person's needs plays an important role in disagreements. Too often when we are in conflict, we want only to win. We want to be right. We feel slighted or offended by the other person's words or behavior and want the other person to change what they are doing that we see as wrong. We don't mind a win-lose scenario so long as we are not on the losing end. It's been said that people don't mind not winning as much as they mind losing. That's because losing is an affront to our self-identity. This attitude, however, is rooted purely in reactivity and does nothing to help relationships or create good feelings or understanding between people. Whenever there is a loser in a personal relationship, alienation is a result and some degree of closeness is lost.

So what does it mean to win in a conflict? Despite a belief to the contrary, winning doesn't always mean being right. Winning means having your point of view heard and your needs or desires addressed in a way that preserves your dignity and shows respect for your boundaries. To fully understand what winning in a conflict looks like, we'll need to do a quick refresher on basic human needs and boundaries.

Reviewing Needs and Boundaries

All of us have needs, from the basic physical requirements of food and shelter to the emotional and psychological desire for affection, acceptance, independence, and so on. Living harmoniously with others requires balancing needs—and that's hard to do in a household with even two people—much less three, four, or more. Suppose you are on the phone with a client, and your son Joe wants you to look at something he has created. Do you interrupt your call to give him the attention he wants? Suppose your husband comes home from work wanting nothing more than a few quiet minutes telling you about his day, and your daughter Sally is expecting dinner now. Whose needs do you satisfy? The answers to such questions are seldom cut and dried—in many ways, every situation is unique. But being present, mindful, and aware, and having a loving intention toward everyone—yourself included—will go a long way toward choosing behavior that is thoughtful rather than reactive.

By staying attuned to your inner world, you can recognize what your emotions are saying about your own needs. By respecting those needs and describing them to your family, you teach others to respect your needs. You also invite them to share their own needs openly and honestly, and you provide a model for doing that in a way that does not include anger and blaming. Here are some of the fundamental needs virtually all people share:

Respect, respect, respect: Respect is the basis of an emotionally healthy relationship. Without it, a lot of anger is
generated because a boundary gets crossed. Think of all
the anger that has been generated over the years because
some brother or sister had the audacity to enter a sibling's
room—enough power to light Chicago. Another key principle here is that while behavior may be objectionable,
people never are. Respect preserves important boundaries and a healthy sense of self.
Time and attention: One of the most powerful ways to show
your love for others is by giving them time and attention.
Being the focus of your full presence makes people feel

important, valued, nurtured, seen, and accepted for who they are.

Affection: Affection is the physical and verbal display of our feelings of love and connectedness—hugging, kissing, throwing an arm around the shoulder or waist, patting a cheek—and simply saying, "I love you." This can be part of passionate foreplay, but simple affection should have its own place in your relationship.

Approval: We grow up seeking approval from our parents, and whether or not we get it, we continue to need approval and support from the people whose opinion we value. Simple compliments are a good place to start.

Security, predictability, and consistency: We all need predictability and consistency: a secure base while we cope with the changes life throws our way. Our closest relationships should provide this base of support for us, and in turn, we need to be there reliably for the people we say we love.

Autonomy and control: No matter how close our relationship becomes, we need to maintain a separate identity, a sense of self, and we should understand and accept that others in our lives will have their own priorities that may occasionally take precedence over us.

To create loving relationships, we must always approach our conflicts with the intention of achieving a win-win outcome, one in which both sides come away feeling positive about the exchange.

The Phenomenon of Counterwill

When we resolve conflicts with respect for both parties' needs, we also avoid triggering counterwill, the innate human resistance to being controlled. No one likes to be forced, cajoled, manipulated, or otherwise coerced into behaving a certain way.

Although the resistance may not be expressed openly, it still remains, generating anger that may also be suppressed. There's no happy ending to this trail.

Real change happens only when people act from an inner motivation and desire to do so: You can change yourself, but you cannot change other people, no matter how close you are. When you find yourself in conflict, others need to know that you want them to get their needs met, too. Beyond not meaning to harm them, you must show them that you love them—you want the best for them. This takes a great deal of mindfulness and commitment to do, especially in charged situations, which is why the emotional work of clearing out any stores of old anger you might have is so important to your interactions with others. Without that emotional freedom, it will be much, much harder to connect.

With emotional freedom and good intent, you're more than halfway to healthy relationships. To get you the rest of the way, you need consistent mindfulness of yourself and your interactions and a strong set of practical strategies and skills that promote healthy relationships. Though entire books are dedicated to the teaching of these strategies and the building of these skills, the next chapter will give you an introduction to them to get you well on your way.

CHAPTER 11

Transforming Anger Into Communication

In the same way that mindful anger can bring us emotional freedom, mindfulness in our relationships can bring us the intimacy and support we are seeking from each other. The connection between the two areas makes sense: Difficulties in our relationships often generate anger, and reactive approaches to anger are a sure way to torpedo relationships. Although our focus in this book is on anger, we've inevitably observed a lot of relationships, particularly situations in which two people disagree or have conflicting goals. In every case, mindfulness offers a productive alternative.

In Chapter 1, for example, we met Beth—an anger withholder—who quietly put up with her husband Norm's ongoing efforts to meet the demands of his ex-wife, Karen. If Beth had acknowledged her anger instead of suppressing it, she might have engaged her new husband in a conversation about the time and caring she needed from him—not a blaming conversation. Mindful of his concerns, she might have opened the door for Norm to discuss the conflict he certainly must have felt between his feelings for Beth and his connection to Karen and their children. At the same time, she could have told him how much she missed his time and attention. As a result, Beth and Norm might have grown closer by sharing this problem together. And who knows—one outcome might have been that

Karen would release what appeared to be her lingering attachment to Norm, allowing her to pursue new partners and a new family circle. More love for everyone.

In Chapter 6, we met Ginny, who assumed that her friend Alice's lunchtime distraction was a signal that their friendship was failing—that Alice no longer cared about her or valued her company. Had Ginny attended mindfully to Alice's behavior instead of jumping to conclusions—if she had focused on Alice as well as herself—she might have asked what was troubling her friend. Perhaps Alice was just having a bad day at the office, or she might have welcomed the chance to discuss more complicated problems—even difficulties she was having with Ginny. However it turned out, they would have both walked away feeling a closer bond.

As these illustrations show, the key to getting what you need or want often is communication: articulating what you need and what the person could do to help fulfill your need, while also attending to the other person's desires and feelings. If we feel vulnerable or insecure in asking for what we need or want, we may do it in a way that puts off the other party: becoming demanding, forceful, or demoralizing in our communication, or doing it in an indirect, passive-aggressive way that frustrates and annoys the other person. Of course, these tactics often get us the opposite of cooperation because they infringe on the other person's sense of self or make him or her feel guilty. The most productive discussions are alert to the other person's perspective on the conflict and sensitive to the person's needs.

This strategy can be useful in the most mundane setting. Not long ago, I learned that I would need some dental work. Not having dental insurance, I asked the office manager to give me an estimate of the cost. I was blown away. Thoughts and feelings rushed in—How could I afford this? Where would the money come from? Why were they doing this to me?—I'm sure you know how it goes.

Before I could let my feelings overflow into a loud protest, however, I took a couple of deep breaths and thought. Like me, the dentist was a professional who deserved a fair fee for his expertise and his services. Rather than getting angry or spending the time to see if I could find a better price someplace else, I had a chat with the office manager. This is an awful lot of money, I explained, and I don't have insurance. Was there anything they could do to help? My response earned me a substantial discount.

If you've been letting your anger explode or stuffing it inside, it may take you a little time to convert your communication patterns, but there's an enormous payoff in terms of improved connections with important others in our lives.

THE FACTS ABOUT COMMUNICATION STYLES

There are four basic communication styles, all of them related to how we respond to the angry feelings life inevitably generates. The first three styles also tend to generate anger in the people who are on the receiving end.

Aggressive communicators: Characteristic of anger dumpers, this style of communication may feature screaming or insults, but the aggression goes beyond volume. Aggressive communicators want to dominate their environment and everyone in it. Often, no one else gets to talk. Like anger dumping, aggressive communicating is basically reactive. Despite—or perhaps because of—their low self-esteem, aggressive communicators often bluster their way through conversations, blaming others for any disagreement, and pressing their case until the other party surrenders.

Passive communicators: Characteristic of anger withholders, this style of communication is almost the exact opposite.

Passive communicators rarely have much to say, and those few words often involve apologizing. Aside from an occasional explosion, they don't speak their mind or stand up for their rights, and insults or grievances will go unremarked. Their body language is withdrawn, too, and they may avoid eye contact.

Passive-aggressive communicators: This is another communication style that suits anger withholders. While passive-aggressive communicators will go out of their way to avoid confrontation, their anger may reveal itself subtly in criticism or sarcasm. They may hide mean words behind an innocent smile or mutter their remarks so quietly you hardly catch a word.

Assertive communicators: For those who have learned the techniques of mindful anger, assertive communication becomes an option with many advantages. Rooted in the present and aware of their emotions and those of others, assertive communicators approach their interactions in a spirit of collaboration. They express their needs directly and clearly, but they also listen to others with a genuine interest in their goals and opinions.

As you achieve the emotional freedom resulting from productive approaches to anger, assertive communication becomes an option that will allow you to improve the outcome of all your interactions and bring a new intimacy to your closest relationships.

Assertiveness Checklist

- Slow down: Take a cleansing breath or two, and speak when you are calm.
- Fill in the blanks. No one knows what you're thinking

and feeling until you tell them. Even people who love you can't read your mind.

- Be confident. You have a valid point of view that needs to be heard.
- Replace sweeping statements with specifics. Instead of saying, "You never do any work around the house," say, "I need help with household chores, especially cleaning up the kitchen after dinner." Avoid the words *always* and *never*.
- Use I statements—notice the previous example.
- Before you speak, recall your deepest feelings for this person. Keep this in mind so that your voice and body language do not reveal hidden anger.
- Know when to stop. The other person deserves the same opportunity to speak and to be heard.

Poet Maya Angelou said, "We do the best we can with what we know, and when we know better, we do better." The good news about assertive communication is that you can start using it at any time: No matter how long you've practiced unproductive styles of communication, it's never too late to get immediate results. Although a reservoir of anger and resentment may exist in your relationships, you can break the dam that is holding all that unproductive emotion. As you change the way you approach the important others in your life, they will gradually learn to trust that you have changed, and new directions become possible.

Assertive communication delivers two important messages, beyond the words that we actually say. First, it gives us a sense that we are acting from a position of power, and it tells other people that we are strong and self-confident. Second, it expresses an interest in hearing—and truly listening to—

what other people have to say. That way we can be sure we are responding to accurate information about what they think and feel, instead of making assumptions based on distorted past experiences.

THE FUNDAMENTALS OF ASSERTIVE COMMUNICATION

Best of all, assertive communication is something you can learn, and you don't have to be school age to enroll in the class. You may have grown up with ineffective ways to deal with your emotions and interact with others, but you can still learn to share your thoughts and feelings in a straightforward way, while approaching others with empathy and compassion. Some basic principles can form the basis of your lessons in this new personal skill.

Aiming for a Win-Win

Much of this book has focused on identifying the sources of your anger and then expressing your needs and boundaries clearly. To build your assertive communication skills, you also need to identify and consider the needs and boundaries of the other person engaged in the exchange.

You may have in mind a vacation in Italy—you've practically got the agenda worked out in your imagination. All you need is the tickets. The only problem is that this year is your partner's 25th high school reunion, and he has always looked forward to this chance to return to the past. Separate vacations won't work because an important element of your partner's return to yesteryear is taking you along to show off. Through assertive communication, you can reach a solution that makes both of you feel satisfied and respected, with neither person feeling that they've sacrificed or surrendered.

Although sometimes priorities have to be juggled, everyone's needs should be honored. Only when both partners are healthy and happy is it possible to have a harmonious relationship. The alternative is resentment and bitterness, which create more—you guessed it—anger.

Invite Emotional Sharing

It's a common complaint among partners who live together: Someone comes home cranky or withdrawn. The reactive response is to assume that the low spirits have to do with you or the home environment. The assertive solution is so simple: Ask what's wrong, not in a challenging way but with real concern.

Our culture has a built-in phobia of negative emotions: We admire the brave souls who bear their pain or grief or disappointment with a smile and swallow their tears. We don't want to know how they actually feel, for fear that their display of emotions might trigger our own. It makes us uncomfortable. In close partnerships, we also may fear what they will say if we ask what's wrong: What if it's us? So we let these moments pass in silence rather than opening the door to potential conflict and the hurt it may inflict.

The result is isolation. The poet John Donne famously said that "no man is an island," but in fact we are all cast away on the shore of our selfhood unless we reach out to others. Communication is the bridge that forms that connection. It's not hard to throw out that lifeline: "You seem a little sad today. If you want to share, I'd be happy to listen." "It must be hard to adapt to the loss of your father. How are you doing?"

Opening the door to let others tell us their thoughts and emotions is the only valid way to connect. Otherwise, we're imagining their internal life or making assumptions based on behavior.

Learn to Listen; Listen to Understand

You may remember this from classroom discussions when you were in school. While one student is talking, several others are waving their arms eagerly, hoping to be the next person to get the floor. And too often, when they do, their remark diverts the conversation from an interesting thread. It's the problem with Web comments, too. Hardly anyone bothers to scroll through the e-conversation, so a lot of entries are repetitive or off the point.

This happens when people are focused only on what they have to say rather than attending to the other parties in the conversation. It's an all-too-common occurrence, even in the most intimate exchanges between two people in a quiet room.

Barring physical deafness, we hear in spite of ourselves: Our ears gather up the sound impulses, then pass them along to the nerve endings of the inner ear. Our brain translates the sounds into words, but that's where it ends unless we choose to listen. That's a much more profound activity in which we muster our memories, feelings, and knowledge about the person and the situation to understand the meaning behind the words.

True listening also involves empathy, which I explore next. I've put listening first because it provides the raw materials that make empathy possible. Another's words are our bridge to accessing that person. And keep in mind that the same is true in reverse. In many ways, our words are crucial to what people in our lives know about us.

Here are some tips for becoming an effective listener:

- Focus on the present. You can't listen if you're worrying about what happened earlier in the day or where you're supposed to be next. If necessary, ask the person to wait while you clear your mind.
- Lower your defenses. Postpone a conversation until your anger or other emotions are processed and released.

- Remember your intent. What are your long-term intentions, your deepest feelings about the other person? Keep these positive feelings in your heart as you talk. Words and gestures that reflect these feelings will help the two of you remember the larger context of your current conflict.
- Look for the connections. Instead of focusing on your disagreements, look at the common threads and try to weave them together into a resolution.
- Repeat what you hear. From time to time, repeat your partner's message in your own words. That way you can be sure you're interpreting correctly, and you also give the other a chance to modify his or her position.

Effective listening helps you achieve empathy: the closest possible understanding of what's in your partner's heart.

Practice Empathy

Put yourself in someone else's shoes. That's the phrase we often use when we're talking about empathy. I think about the classic love song—I can't quote the lyrics but you know how it goes: When someone's under your skin and deep in your heart, they're really a part of you.

This level of empathy may not be achievable—or even desirable—with everyone in your life, but it's an important goal for those who are closest to you. At a simple level, empathy is seeing the world from another's point of view. Empathy can go much deeper, however, beyond merely sharing others' perspectives to caring as much about their well-being as you care about our own. One characteristic of relationships lacking empathy is that you assume the other person has the same needs and boundaries as you do and experiences life in the same way. This approach won't get you far: Very quickly, you'll hit a bump where you find that he or she is not what you imagined and doesn't always share your preferences or opinions. You love the intimacy of independent films, and she can't wait for the next summer blockbuster; you long for sushi, but the thought of raw fish turns his stomach. More profoundly, your attachment to religion is a cornerstone of your life, and the other sees the church as an obsolete institution. Relationships can crash because of these kinds of differences, but empathy can create a bridge and generate mutual respect. Friendships in particular are often based on a shared space or activity. How many of your high school or college friends are still in your life 10 years later? You may think you're really best pals with your golfing buddy, but what if an injury puts him or her on the sideline?

Empathy—developed through regularly listening to the other person's thoughts and feelings—helps to build both a closeness and a respect for his or her individuality. It's an important element of assertive communication, and you can learn how to make it part of your life.

EXERCISE: TRYING ON ANOTHER'S SKIN

1. Think about a partner, friend, family member, or coworker.
2. What makes him happy? How does he act when he's happy? Are there words or gestures he uses to indicate his mood?
3. What makes her angry? How does she show her anger— or how can you tell even when she doesn't show it?
4. Describe his favorite foods, music, books, movies.
5. What activities does she enjoy? Is she good at what she does? Does she need to excel, or is she content just doing it?
6. What does he like about you? What do you think he finds irritating?

7. With this information, think about what you could say or do to enhance her life.

8. In a close relationship, you might write down the answers to these questions and share with the other person. See how close you are to getting it right.

Empathy Checklist

- Focus your attention on the person who is talking. Keep your hands in your lap or on the table. Don't fiddle.

- Indicate that you're listening: Meet the person's eye as he or she speaks, nod when you understand, touch a hand, or use another gesture to indicate your connection.

- Show your respect; hear the person out without sarcasm or rejection. If your anger increases, ask for a break so that you can approach it mindfully.

- Repeat what your partner says in your own words, or ask questions if you're not clear about his or her meaning.

- Validate the other's emotions. Even if you don't agree with an opinion, you can acknowledge the person's right to his or her feelings.

Communicate How You Feel

Being in touch with how everyone feels is an important part of assertive communication. Listening to learn and understand and having empathy don't mean that you dismiss how you yourself feel. The purpose of this book has been to give you the tools and inspiration you need to become aware of your feelings and needs so that you can make effective choices to take care of yourself. This next skill is key for communicating what you want, need, or feel without blaming, shaming, or otherwise putting the other person down. I'm of course referring to the classic communication skill of using I statements.

Suppose one partner has suggested having dinner out. Here are four different ways to respond.

1. Aggressive: "You're always trying to duck cooking by going to a restaurant. Why don't you just fix something?"
2. Passive: "We can go."
3. Passive-aggressive: "If you really want to eat out, I'll go along. I suppose we can afford it."
4. Assertive: "I'm feeling a little queasy this evening, and I would rather stay home."

Although the speaker may not mean to control or criticize, using *you* is often an effort to control or criticize. Notice how the aggressive speaker quickly turns the invitation into an opportunity to place blame. While the passive and passive-aggressive speakers agree to go along, their reluctance hidden, the assertive speaker takes responsibility. Let's look at some more examples of how using *I* instead of *you* can change the impact of words, even those that convey a negative message.

- "Your comments about my outfit were really rude. You made me look like a fool in front of your family."

versus

- "I'm feeling angry about our visit to your family. To hear negative remarks about my appearance embarrassed me."

- "If you don't know how to do something, you ought to say so up front. You've made a mess here, and it's going to take me forever to clean up."

versus

- "I didn't understand that you were having trouble getting this done. Let me show you now so you'll know the next time."

Learn to Negotiate

At least when we start cooking, we usually use a cookbook. Even as our skills expand beyond boiling an egg or microwaving a frozen dinner, we often look to experts or professionals to develop those skills and learn about new ingredients or approaches.

There are recipes for resolving conflict, too, and they might be useful to you as you begin to work your way toward assertive communication in your relationship. One strategy, for example, is to limit your focus in a conflict to only what you can and will do to resolve the problem. Each party reflects on the issue between them, takes responsibility for his or her role in it, and describes the steps he or she will take to resolve the problem. Participants don't point fingers or tell the other person what to do. It's a strategy that generates mutual respect instead of anger. Keep in mind that this will feel very foreign at first. It's the opposite of what we're inclined to do, which is to get defensive and blame. The following exercise will give you a little practice so you can begin to adjust to this very important skill.

EXERCISE: FOCUSING ON WHAT YOU CAN DO

1. Think about a recent conflict you had with your partner, a friend, family member, or coworker.
2. What was the disagreement about?
3. Now, from your own realm of responsibility, identify the

steps you might take to solve the problem. Remember, you can't ask the other person to change; you must focus solely on what you can and will do to make things better.

4. Then, if you'd like, share this strategy with the other person and invite him or her to participate with you in getting your conflict resolved. Remind him or her that each of you can only state what you yourselves will do rather than expecting change from the other person.

Say You're Sorry

It's bound to happen. With all your good intentions, you're going to say or do something that you recognize as hurtful. The old maxim from a sentimental movie of the 1970s just isn't so: Love does not mean never having to say you're sorry. Love is accepting responsibility for the offending action and saying you're sorry over and over, if necessary. Putting yourself in the other person's shoes is a good first step.

We've all been on the other side of the net, the one who received the emotional pain or disappointment. Most likely, we've looked for an apology. Why? We need to know that the offending person acknowledges our pain and his or her role in causing it. And the apology has to be sincere, or it just makes the situation worse. A proper apology, however, is like a healing balm applied to a burn. It takes out the sting, and the other's touch soothes and calms us.

Now put yourself back in the offender's seat. Here's how to make sure that when you apologize, you do it right.

- Be genuinely sorry for what you said or did.
- Let the person know you take responsibility for making it right.
- Promise to do your best to avoid repeating the offense.

- Tell the person how much you love and value him or her—nothing may be more important.
- Ask for forgiveness.
- Keep your promise with improved behavior.

Mindful attitudes about yourself and your relationship will reduce the amount of hurt you cause, intentionally or not. In addition, when everyone is listened to, heard, and treated with respect, all parties will be more inclined to apologize for recognized injustices and will want to correct course. This is the beautiful by-product of empathy—when we understand how other people feel, we feel remorseful when we cause them frustration or pain. This won't happen if we aren't listening to our own feelings, especially our anger, and if we're not listening to those who are close to us.

LIKE ANGER, CONFLICT CAN BE GOOD

The startling premise of this book is that anger is good—it's your friend; it can transform your life. The same is true of conflict. The only way—repeat, the only way—to build strong and lasting relationships is to use conflict as a way to learn about each other, to embrace the real person, and to grow in intimacy with each other. Assertive communication is the means to reach this goal. It allows you to view confrontation as an opportunity to identify and heal past emotional wounds and to bond with the people who are important to us.

How to Have a Civilized and Productive Quarrel

Following these guidelines will help you to discuss your differences quietly, and it will improve your chances of reaching a successful conclusion.

- Agree to a time and place for the discussion, a place where you will be alone together and uninterrupted for at least a half hour.
- Leave cell phones, tablets, and other electronic distractions in another space. Clear your mind of competing concerns, as well.
- No blame or criticism. Stick to how you're feeling and what you're thinking. Inform, don't assume.
- Take turns speaking. To ensure that each person's turn is respected, pass an object back and forth if necessary. The one holding the object is the one who speaks. There should be no response until the speaker stops. If there's a dominant partner, bring an egg timer and allot a specific interval for each person.
- No shouting. If the volume starts to rise—or anger seems to be building—take a mutual time-out until both persons have had time to examine their anger and respond mindfully.
- Look for agreement. Keep an eye out for commonalities as the discussion goes forward. You might even write them on sticky notes, so that you can see your progress over the course of the discussion.
- Conclude with an expression of love. Even if you don't find a solution in your first discussion, you love each other, don't you? Let that show in your words and gestures as you move to implement your mutual decision or set another time to discuss the problem.

If you grew up in a household where conflict always led to open expressions of anger, even violence, it may take you some time to accept this. The same is true if your family dealt with conflict by always conceding to the strongest personality and avoiding discussing—or even acknowledging—differences at any cost. Nevertheless, you can learn another way to approach conflict and reap the fruits of your efforts.

Anger and conflict are intertwined, like the proverbial chicken and egg. The work you put into changing your response to anger and dealing with it productively will help you to communicate assertively with everyone in your life, from the counter clerk at the local coffeehouse to the partner who shares your most intimate moments. Making a habit of mindful anger will foster mindful relationships, and vice versa.

You can do this. You can start now.

The New You

Congratulations. You have reached the end of this book. By now you should feel lighter and freer, having unloaded a lot of old, toxic energy that was weighing you down and keeping you stuck. You have also gained great insight into yourself: understanding your anger and the purpose it serves, becoming more aware of your needs and how to meet them, and acquiring the tools for facing and working through new issues as they arise. With this newfound strength and wisdom, you have achieved an emotional freedom that will enhance your enjoyment of life and your connection with others.

Turning the tools of mindfulness to your relationships, you have also learned new strategies for dealing with the conflicts that are so often associated with anger. Our interactions with others are a common source of anger triggers, and when we approach others with anger in our hearts, conflict is never far away. By approaching conflicts mindfully with assertive communication and empathy for the other person, we can achieve resolutions in which both parties are the winners.

Indeed, we all are covered by the same basic emotional bill of rights. The first principle of this bill of rights is that you have a right to your feelings. The second principle is that none of your feelings are wrong; they simply exist as part of life. And the third principle—the last one—is that your feelings are messengers, delivering valuable information to you. One of the main purposes of this book is to encourage you to listen to the messages your feelings try to deliver. This is important because your feelings are there to guide you, teach you about yourself, and help you navigate life so you can achieve more of what you want to experience.

Achieving emotional freedom, you have the strength to respect the same rights for other people in your life. Both elements are crucial to reaching your full potential as a human being—there's scientific evidence that the brain needs self-reflection and close personal relationships to complete its development. But you won't need science to tell you that mindful anger and its outcomes have an enormously beneficial payoff.

Since my breakthrough, I have spent 30 years or more in open and caring relationships. I have a successful 20-year marriage to a man I love, and I also cherish my stepchildren and grandchildren. The more adversity I have experienced, the more vulnerability I've allowed myself to feel. My friendships have become stronger and happier. I live authentically in a way that was completely foreign to me as a younger adult.

I reflect with sadness on the very different life course followed by Christina, who appeared in Chapter 7. It's bad enough that she suffered the loss of her mother when she was only 9 years old. Even worse, no one in her family was able to help her handle her grief. The worst was that this wound festered throughout her life, short-circuiting all the relationships that, although some would inevitably have brought her grief, would also have enriched her days.

This unhappy ending is not set in stone for the many of us who begin life in families that provide poor models. Perhaps your childhood failed to give you an understanding of the role of anger and emotions in your life. Perhaps you still bear the wounds of childhood abuse or neglect. You may not have gained the communication skills to present yourself with confidence or to interact with others compassionately and collaboratively. All of that is in the past.

The future begins now. I hope that somewhere in this book you have found the word or phrase or insight that will open you to change: mind and body and heart. Whatever your circumstances, nothing can be gained by locking away your anger and all the painful memories surrounding it. Most important, when you unlock the anger, you will also find yourself unlocking opportunities for love in your life. I wish you all the best on this journey.

Bibliography

Brandt, Andrea. *8 Keys to Eliminating Passive-Aggressiveness*. New York: Norton, 2013.

Casarjian, Robin. *Forgiveness: A Bold Choice for a Peaceful Heart*. New York: Bantam, 1992.

Cunningham, Aimee. "The Pleasure of Revenge." *Scientific American*, November 17, 2004. http://www.scientificamerican.com/article.cfm?id=the-pleasure-of-revenge

DeFoore, William Gray. *Anger: Deal With It, Heal With It, Stop It From Killing You*. Deerfield Beach, FL: Health Communications, 1991.

Fischer, Kristen. "Ticked Off? Your Serotonin Could Be Low." She Knows, November 3, 2011. http://www.sheknows.com/health-and-wellness/articles/845939/ticked-off-your-serotonin-could-be-low.

Kurtz, Ron. *Body-Centered Psychotherapy: The Hakomi Method*. Mendocino, CA: LifeRhythm, 1990.

Lee, John. *The Anger Solution: The Proven Method for Achieving Calm and Developing Healthy, Lasting Relationships*. Cambridge, MA: Da Capo, 2009.

Luhn, Rebecca R. *Managing Anger: Methods for a Happier and Healthier Life*. Menlo Park, CA: Crisp, 1992.

Marshall, Marvin. *Parenting Without Stress: How to Raise Responsible Kids While Keeping a Life of Your Own*. Los Alamitos, CA: Piper, 2010.

Maslin, Bonnie. *The Angry Marriage: Overcoming the Rage, Reclaiming the Love.* New York: Hyperion, 1994.

Middleton-Moz, Jane, Lisa Tener, and Peaco Todd. *The Ultimate Guide to Transforming Anger: Dynamic Tools for Healthy Relationships.* Deerfield Beach, FL: Health Communications, 2004.

Potter-Efron, Ronald T., and Patricia S. Potter-Efron. *Letting Go of Anger: The Eleven Most Common Anger Styles and What to Do About Them,* 2nd ed. Oakland, CA: New Harbinger, 2006.

Robinson, Bryan E. *Chained to the Desk: A Guidebook for Workaholics, Their Partners and Children, and the Clinicians Who Treat Them,* 2nd ed. New York: NYU Press, 2007.

Siegel, Daniel J. *The Mindful Brain: Reflection and Attunement in the Cultivation of Well-Being.* New York: Norton, 2007.

Siegel, Daniel J. *Mindsight: The New Science of Personal Transformation.* New York: Bantam, 2010.

Stiffelman, Susan. *Parenting Without Power Struggles: Raising Joyful, Resilient Kids While Staying Cool, Calm and Connected.* Garden City, NY: Morgan James, 2010.

Susman, Ed. "Anger Drives Heart Attacks but Laughter May Be Antidote." Everyday Health, August 28, 2011. http://www.everydayhealth.com/heart-health/0829/anger-drives-heart-attacks-but-laughter-may-be-antidote.aspx.

Viorst, Judith. *Necessary Losses: The Loves, Illusions, Dependencies, and Impossible Expectations That All of Us Have to Give Up in Order to Grow.* New York: Free Press, 1998.

Whitfield, Charles L. *Boundaries and Relationships: Knowing, Protecting, and Enjoying the Self.* Deerfield Beach, FL: Health Communications, 1993.

Index